Christian Braun

Jiu-Jitsu Training

Meyer & Meyer Sport

British Library Cataloguing in Publication Data
A catalogue record for this book is available from the British Library

Jiu-Jitsu Training
Oxford: Meyer & Meyer Sport (UK) Ltd., 2006
ISBN 978-1-84126-179-9

2nd Edition 2007
Aachen, Adelaide, Auckland, Budapest, Graz, Indianapolis, Johannesburg,
New York, Olten (CH), Oxford, Singapore, Toronto
Member of the World
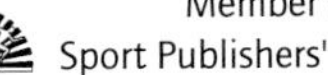
Sport Publishers' Association (WSPA)
www.w-s-p-a.org
Printed and bound by: Burg Verlag Gastinger GmbH, Germany
ISBN 978-1-84126-179-9
E-Mail: verlag@m-m-sports.com
www.m-m-sports.com

Index

Foreword

Over time, Jiu-Jitsu has adopted defense techniques that emanate from Judo, Karate and Aikido as well as from other Martial Arts forms including the Philippine systems (Arnis, Kali and Eskrima), the Brazilian system (Brazilian Jiu-Jitsu, Luta-Livre), the Thai system (Muay Thai) and Jeet Kune Do.

Because of this, in my opinion, Jiu-Jitsu represents one of the most complete Martial Arts systems on offer at the moment. It contains self-defense techniques for all reach distances (for kicking, boxing, trapping, throwing and groundwork) as well as defense against attacks by opponents using weapons.

From experience gained in fighting 'without rules' (Vale Tudo) it has been established that a Martial Art system without groundwork techniques is generally non-effective. The 'complete' fighter has to be good in all areas. A modern expression for this is "cross-fighting". Jiu-Jitsu is more than just "cross-fighting", because it also includes defense against attacks with weapons.

For me, Jiu-Jitsu has the advantage that instruction on the whole is qualitatively very good, and in relation to other types of sports there is a positive acclamation for it. There is a considerable amount of information available both in publications and particularly on the Internet.

Find out for yourself how easy it is to learn about this fascinating sport–just type in 'jiu-jitsu' in any of the search engines and you will be surprised.

May I wish the reader lots of fun when working through this book. As always, I am very happy to help anyone with his or her questions–you can reach me using Christian.Braun@open-mind-combat.com.

Frankenthal, October 2005, Christian Braun
www.open-mind-combat.com

1 Introduction

In this volume, the forms of movement are gone into further. The pupil should now be able to use all that he has learned in the way of Atemi techniques and attacks freely against an attacking opponent and continually be in a situation to improve his position. Training in this field covers not only these facets in a standing position but also in groundwork.

In the breakfall 'school', the pupil will be confronted for the first time with suddenly being brought to the ground (forwards and backwards). Both of these need some getting used to at the beginning. By using the correct preliminary exercises, the pupil will quickly gain confidence. The breakfall techniques learned up till now are used after being tumbled over or being deliberately thrown by the opponent. The pupil must now be able to practice follow on combinations after he has been put down on the ground.

Two immobilization techniques and a further freeing technique expand the pupil's spectrum of knowledge in groundwork. In addition, he will also learn strangleholds and locking techniques in groundwork. In other types of sport one has the expression "submission" e.g., by applying strangleholds and locking techniques the opponent has to be forced to give in. In the first volume, a section entitled "Complex Exercise" was introduced. From practice stemming from this volume, the pupil must be in a position to be able to show he can do one or more throwing techniques against a passive, mobile partner.

"The classic form of exercise from the Philippine system—the 'three-step contact' (also called 'Hubud' in the parent system)—is covered in detail." This form of exercise (drill) schools the pupil's reaction and teaches him, above all else, the ability to be able to come in from the inside to the outside of the opponent quickly and safely, and which is generally a better way for the defender to act. Use of the 'three-step contact' can also be made to effect, for example locking, throwing and Atemi techniques. Also, by using the 'three-step contact' this gives better training for the follow-on on having defended against Atemi techniques. These exercise forms have the advantage that the partner is always sporadically attacking during the drills, and this gives more training time on the requirement to be able to react.

With regards to the Jiu-Jitsu techniques themselves, we must not overlook the very effective technique of the shinbone kick (low kick). The shinbone kick comes from the Muay Thai system.

Similarly the basics of self-defense against stick attacks are covered in detail. Here, the pupil has to learn to defend against 8 stick attacks coming in from various set angles, that is to say he must be at least able to control the arm holding the weapon. In a second step, further disrupting techniques are shown. Further techniques such as disarming are optional. These will be covered in later volumes. Besides the techniques from the Japanese systems, which have stood the test of time, experience from the Philippines systems like Kali, Arnis or Eskrima have now been included.

When one looks at the history of the Philippines, one learns that there is one of the biggest Katana collections (these are the long, slightly curved, sharp sword of the Samurai). The people of the Philippines took them off the Samurai in battle, even though they were only armed with cane sticks and knives. Amongst others the crews of four Spanish men-of-war were slaughtered, despite the fact that the Spanish wore armor and were armed with muskets. Because of this, I believe, that it is well worth while, when one looks closer at the history, to try to adopt the best elements for our own self-defense system. Everything that is old is not necessarily wrong or bad. Some things have just simply been superceded, however, many other things are still just as usable as before.

Followers of the Martial Arts, who have had something to do with the sport Wing Tsun (sometimes spelled differently) or Jeet Kune Do, will have probably noticed that most of the advanced pupils are good at one distance. In their curriculum they speak of "trapping". This is covered in this book in the actions termed as 'follow-on techniques' having defended against an 'Atemi technique'. In my opinion, this is a very interesting theme that should be considered yet even more in Jiu-Jitsu. In the two chapters on 'Follow-on Techniques' and 'Counter Measure Techniques', the pupil will learn more about the locking techniques. In 'Free Self-defense', measures against five different types of hugging holds are set for the pupil.

As a basic marker—in the following chapters the defender is indicated by the letter 'D' and the attacker/opponent 'A'.

2 Forms of Movement (Sabaki)

2.1 Changing stances

Forwards

Backwards

On the spot

2.2 Forms of movement in groundwork

Defense stance

Changing over to the other side

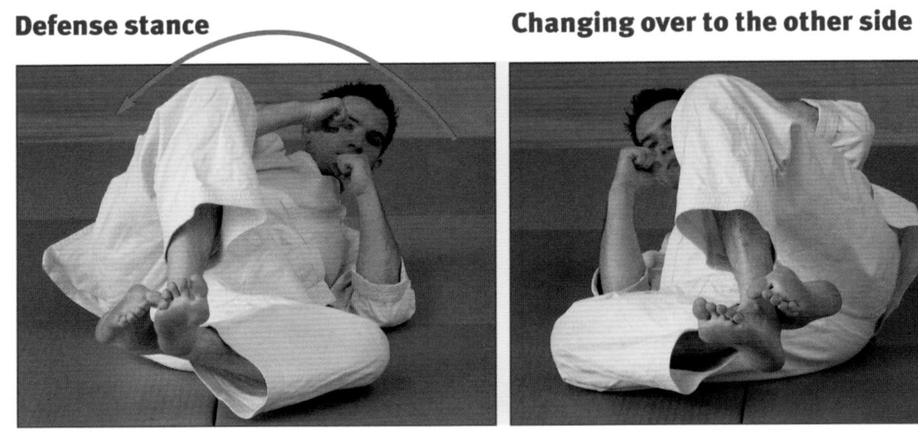

Gliding on the ground

Turning on the ground

Rolling on the ground

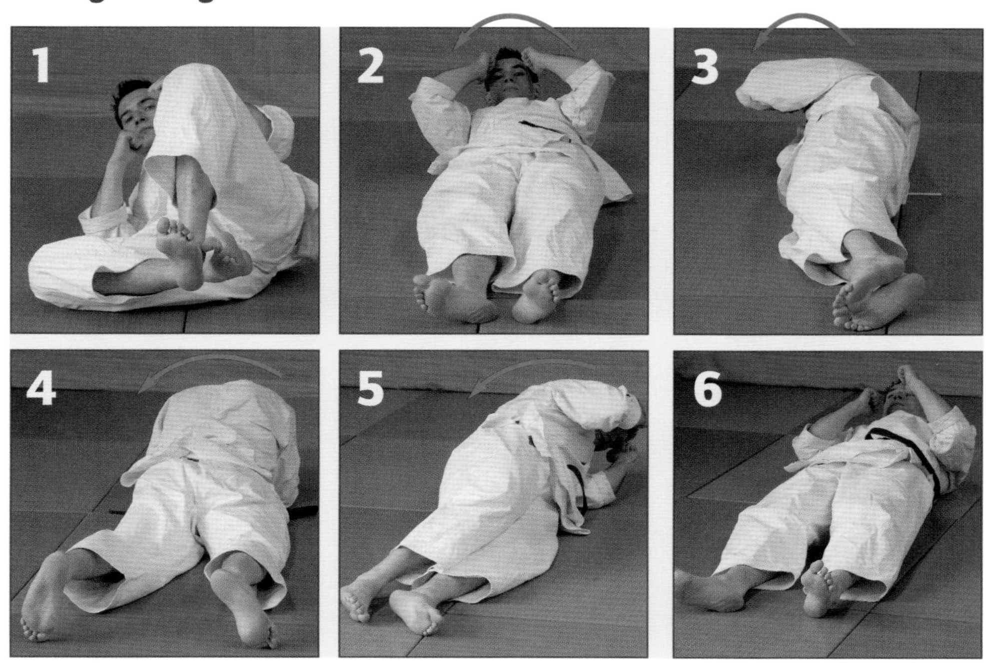

Standing up from the ground

2.3 Free movement forms

- The pupil is attacked by his partner using free Atemi techniques or straight attacks.
- The pupil only uses defense elements of the Jiu-Jitsu Sabaki in combination with passive or active defense techniques.
- The exercise is done first of all standing and then with the defender on the ground.

2.3.1 Movements in the standing position

2.3.2 Movements on the ground

3 Breakfalls (Ukemi)

3.1 Fall forwards

Preliminary exercise from the kneeling position

3.2 Fall backwards

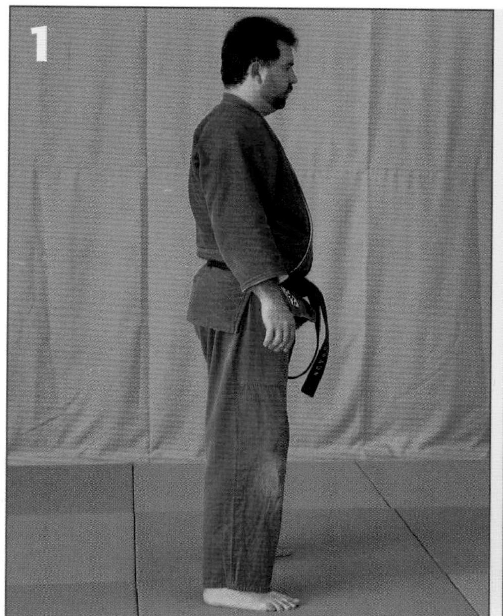

3.3 Rolling over obstacles in the standing position

3.2.1 Forwards

3.2.1 Backwards

3.4 Breakfall techniques with a partner

- The pupil is brought down to the ground by the partner either by being pushed or using any form of throw in any direction towards the ground.

- After having done the appropriate fall technique, the pupil defends himself with any choice of technique.

4 Groundwork Techniques (Ne-waza)

4.1 Holding technique with the opponent on the stomach

- The defender weighs down the opponent who is lying on his stomach with his body.
- The opponent's ability to move is further limited by the defender controlling the opponent's hips with his legs.
- The arms are holding the opponent's arms and/or his head.

D brings both of his legs underneath A's, pushes his right forearm in front of A's neck, places his right hand on A's left biceps with his right hand on A's head. D places his own head on the back of his own left hand and stretches his upper body forwards. In this way a neck lock is applied and a stranglehold is made.

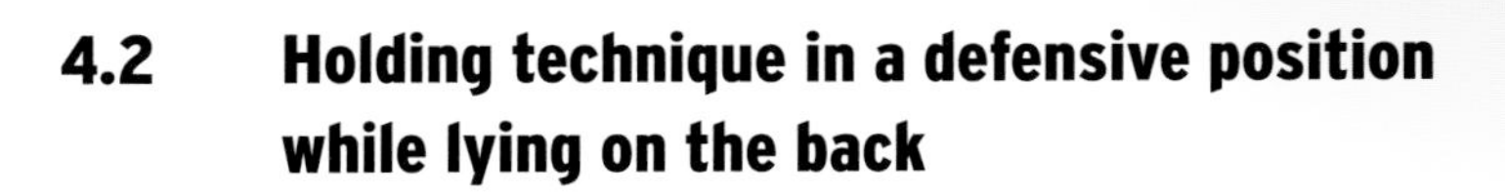

4.2 Holding technique in a defensive position while lying on the back

- The opponent is clamped between the defender's legs while he is lying on his back.
- The arms are holding the opponent's arm and/or his head.

D is holding A in the 'guard' position.
D grabs hold of A's right arm and brings this over to the right-hand side.
The left hand is placed on the nape of A's neck and pins the head to D's body.

4.3 Moving from lying on the back into the upper position

- The defender is in a defensive position lying on his back.
- He is holding the opponent who is kneeling between D's legs.
- By using his body and his extremities he forces the opponent out of the starting position onto his back and holds him then down.

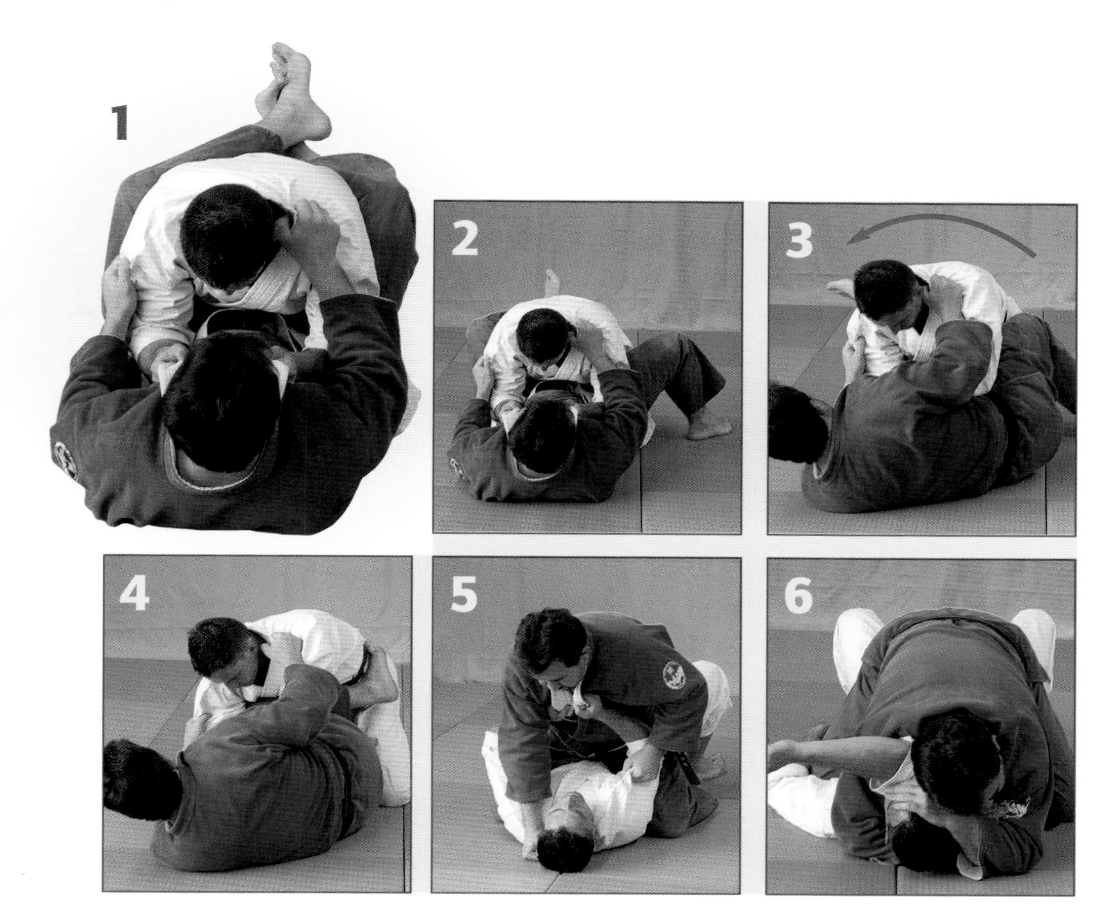

1. D places his right leg out to the side...
2. ...brings his right hip a little out to the side...
3. ...pushes his right knee in front of A's groin/stomach.
D places his left leg on the ground close by A's right leg.
4-6. D now executes a scissors movement while at the same time doing a turning movement with the arms (like driving a car) so that A is brought onto his back.

1. D is controlling A on the ground.
2. D places his right leg out to the side...
3. ...brings his right hip a little out to the sidepushes his right knee in front of A's groin/stomach.
4. D places his left leg on top of A's right leg.
5-6. D now pushes the right leg away to the rear while pulling at the same the right arm forward with his left arm, supporting the turning movement with the right leg...
7-8. ...so that A is brought onto his back.

4.4 Holding techniques for a lock or strangling technique

- The holding techniques covered so far are combined each now with a lock or a strangling technique.
- The pupil must execute each position individually one after the other.

4.4.1 Holding technique in the sideways position

1. D brings his left forearm behind A's head and takes hold of his left hand with his right hand pushing his right elbow at the same time onto A's breastbone.
2. By pulling the head and applying pressure on the breastbone a neck lock is achieved.

1. D is controlling A in sideways grasp.
2. D brings A's right arm inwards with his left arm...
3. ...reaches round A's neck with the right arm and takes hold of his own right hand with his left hand presses the head against A's right upper arm and executes a stranglehold.

4.4.2 Holding technique in the mounted straddle position

1. D is in the straddle position.
2. D brings his right arm underneath A's head and places the right hand on his left biceps...
3. ...lays the left hand on the right-hand side of A's head with his own right cheek directly on his hand. D hooks both legs under A's and his right shoulder is in front of A's jaw. Now, D pushes himself forwards thus increasing the neck lock and the pressure on A's jawbone.

1. D is in the straddle position.
   D holds down A's right arm with his left arm...
2. ...places his left foot directly next to the left side of A's head...
3. ...slips his right knee over A's left upper arm...
4. ...and ends the combination with a stretched arm lock.

4.4.3 Holding technique in the crossover position

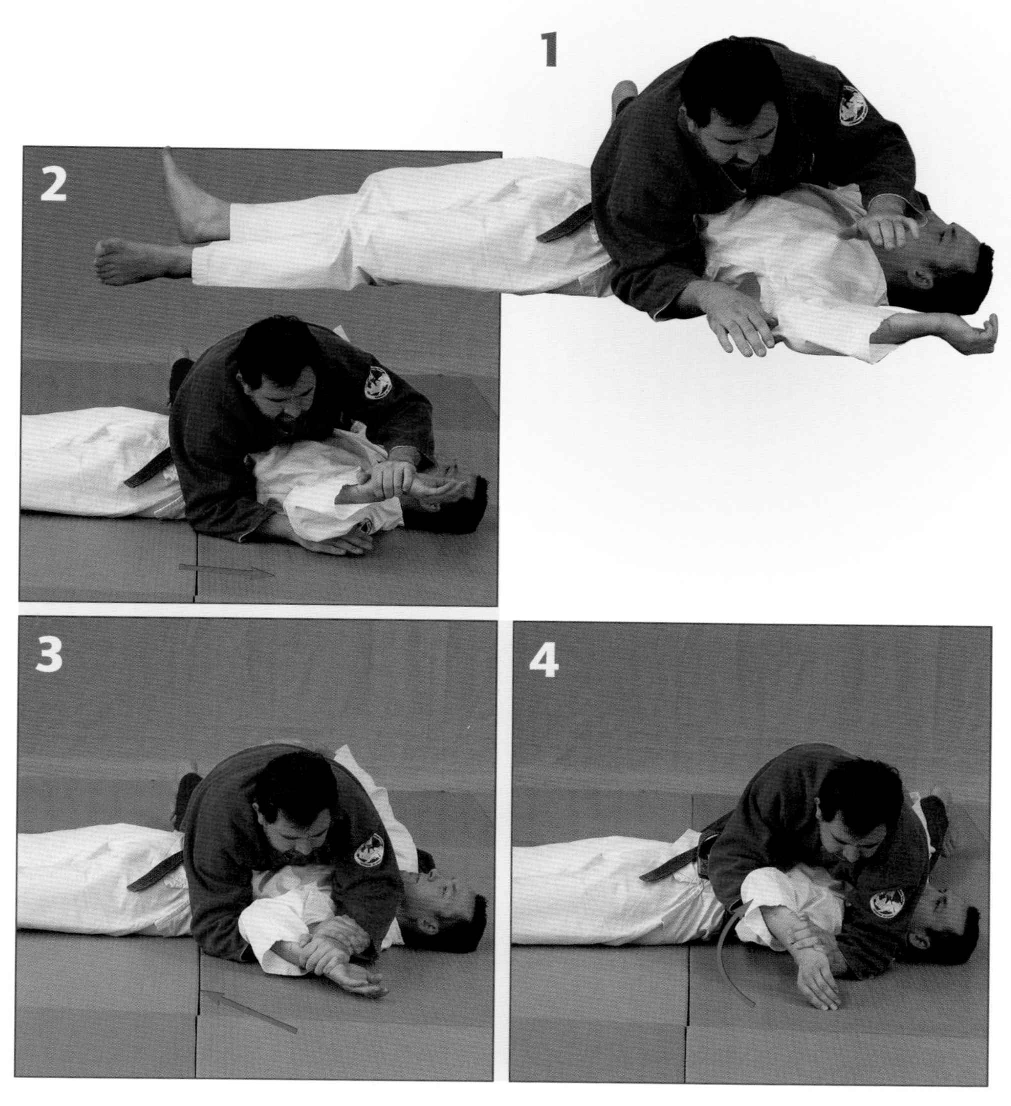

1. A's arm is pointing in the direction of his head.
2. D grabs hold of A's left wrist, pushes his right arm through under A's left arm,
3. takes hold of his own left wrist with the right hand, twists the wrist (as if revving up a motor-bike), pulls A's left elbow in the direction of A's left hip, pins the left hand on the ground...
4. ...and lifts A's left arm with the right forearm resulting in a bent arm lock.

4.4.4 Holding technique with the opponent on his stomach

1

1. D pushes both of his legs underneath A's legs and pulls his legs close around A's upper body...
2. pushes the right arm underneath A's neck taking hold of his own left biceps...
3. ...places the left hand on A's head with his own head on the back of his own left hand and carries out a stranglehold.

1. D pushes both of his legs underneath A's legs and pulls his legs close around A's upper body...
2. ...pushes the right arm underneath A's neck and grips deep into the collar.
   D pulls the collar up round A's neck presses the left hand down on the ground close to the right-hand side of A's neck and carries out a stranglehold this way using the clothing.

4.4.5 Holding technique when on the back and with the opponent between the legs (Guard position)

2. D grabs hold of A's right wrist with his left hand and grips around A's back with his legs...

3. ...lifting the body up and grabbing over A's right arm with the right arm and taking hold of his own left wrist.
4. D rights himself again...
5. ...pushes the hip outwards to gain a better force for the bent arm lock and pushes A's right arm in the direction of A's left shoulder.

1. A is in the frontal guard position.
2. D brings A's right arm onto the right side of his body (in the direction of the groin) and pins the arm with his right hand.
3. Using his left hand, D pins A's head (round the neck behind the right-hand side of A's head so that he cannot stand up).

4-5. Now, D rolls his left hand around A's head and pushes it over to the left side.

6. D turns his body to the right 90° on the ground swings his left leg over A's head...

7. ...brings his right leg very close to A's left arm i.e., the left leg is lying on A's back and the hollow of his own knee is next to A's left arm.

8. D pulls both of his feet up and presses his heels on the ground. Now, D's left hand takes over holding down A's forearm. A's right arm is stretched out with the left arm pinned to D's upper body. The forearm is used because more power can be exerted than when the arm is held with the hand.
D grabs round A's left thigh with his right hand.
By pushing the hips down a side lock (stretched arm lock) is applied.

5 Complex Exercise

5.1 Carrying out a free choice of throwing technique on a moving, but passive partner (repeated several times)

- The pupil gets hold of the moving partner in a standing position.
- Whilst moving the pupil uses one or more throws of his own choice.
- Points to watch for: Economic and controlled movement, use of correct technique, timing, feeling for distance, overview and dynamics.

5.2 Carrying out a free choice of Atemi combinations on a moving, but passive partner

- The pupil carries out at least one Atemi combination on the moving partner (repeated several times).
- The partner offers only passive protection and dodges away.
- Points to watch for: Economic and controlled movement, use of correct technique, timing, feeling for distance, overview and dynamics.

6 Defense Using the Three-step Contact (Hubud)

Against a strike coming in downwards from the outside

- The sequence of movements in the defense is done in the form of an exercise with a partner; the movement between carrying out the defense and the counter-attack should be flowing.

- **Step 1:** Using the opposite arm (with the hand open) contact is made with the opponent's arm, without stopping the arm.
- **Step 2:** The attack is steered over the head from the outside with the other hand. (Variation: The attack is picked up from the inside and steered downwards).

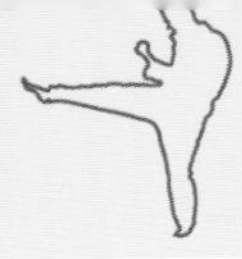

- **Step 3:** Now the hand that is free again takes hold of the opponent's arm from the outside just above the elbow joint.
- The pupil must show he can fluently carry out the defense sequence on any side of his choosing, e.g., against a strike coming down from the outside right. The sequence can be done with variations.

7 Jiu-Jitsu Combination Techniques

The following techniques should be carried out, as chosen by the pupil, using combinations against each type of attack.

The combinations illustrated in this book are only examples and serve to encourage those interested.

7.1 Defensive techniques

7.1.1. Defense techniques blocking with the hand (Uke-waza)

- In defense the flat, tensed hand is used.
- Execution is by choice, with either the flat of the hand, the back of the hand, the outside edge of the hand, the inside edge of the hand or the ball of the hand.
- The defense technique should be combined with the appropriate form of movement.

Technique: Sweeping hand (Parry)

1. A executes a straight, right-handed punch (cross) at D's head.
   D counters with a parry of the left hand to the inside (the fingers are closed!)...

2-3. ...and 'curls' his left hand clockwise round A's upper arm. At the same time, his right hand grabs the nape of A's neck.

4. D executes a kick with his right foot at A's left knee...

5. ...and brings A down with a twisting stretched arm lock onto the ground and uses this technique as an immobilizing grip.

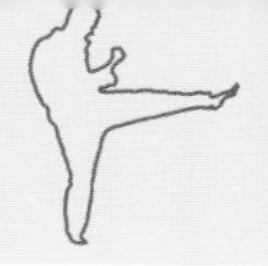

1. A executes a strike with a stick upwards and from the inside.
2. D wards off the strike of the stick downwards to the left and to the outside by using the back of his left hand (fingers are closed)...
3-4. ...and disarms A using the "snake" disarming movement.
5. D places his left hand under the right triceps and executes a strike with the right elbow against the right biceps (Gunting technique).
6. The right hand folds over downwards and brings A's right arm to the right and outside.
7. He follows this up with a left-fisted punch at A's right kidney.
After this, D rubs his right thumb over A's right eye...
8. ...and concludes with a left-fisted punch at A's chin.

1. A executes a right-handed knife attack upwards and outwards towards D's neck.
2. D sweeps the arm with the knife diagonally down to the right and outwards using the right hand (with the fingers closed).
3. D brings his left hand underneath A's right elbow and pushes his right hand or his right arm over A's right arm (to control the arm holding the weapon).
   As he does this, he also delivers a finger/hand jab towards A's eyes.
4. D slips his right hand along the right arm and grabs hold of the ball of the right hand...
5. ...brings the hand inside past his own left arm with his right hand stretches the left arm out lays the blunt, flat side of the knife onto the left biceps...
6. ...pulls the right hand over his own left biceps and thus disarms A.
7. Using his left arm D rolls it over A's right arm...
8. ...and lays it down on A's right elbow and applies a stretched arm lock.

9. D brings A down to the ground by applying pressure on the stretched arm lock...

10. ...and in the ground position, he angles A's right arm round his own left arm and using his right hand, he traps A's left shoulder blade (so that A cannot turn over and execute an elbow strike)...

11. ...and applies pressure with his left against A's levered upper arm forcing A to move forwards and stand up...

12. ...and then executes a crossed-arm grip (bent arm lock to move A about).

1. A executes a semi-circular front kick with his right foot at D's upper body.
D grabs hold of the attacking leg with his right hand (hand sweep) and...

2. directs the foot to the outside so that A is now standing with his back to D.

3-4. D executes a kick with his left shinbone 45° upwards at the rear of A's right thigh...

5. ...and grabs hold of A's head with both hands...

6. ...'jumps' round the attacker and executes a knife-hand strike at A's head with his right hand...

7-8. ...with which he ends the combination.

1. A executes a knife attack upwards to the inside of D's neck.
2. D counters with a spear-hand jab at A's eyes with his right hand, at the same time doing a diagonal sweeping block with his left hand (the fingers are closed).
3. D's right hand grabs hold of A's right hand...
4. ...and pulls it inwards to effect a twisting bent hand lock.
5. The left hand removes the knife.
6. D executes a stretched arm lock to bring A down to the ground and immobilizes him likewise.

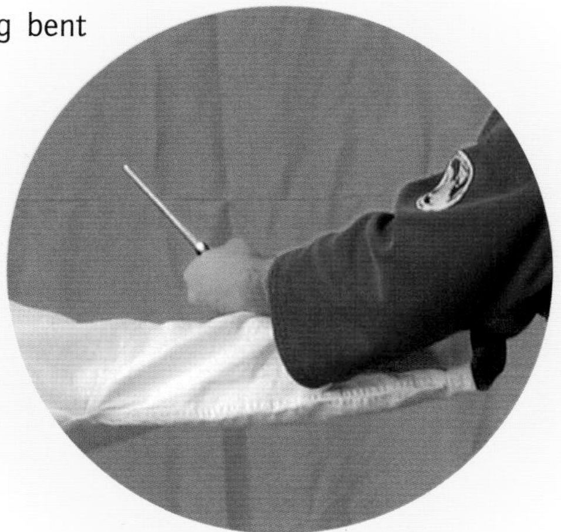

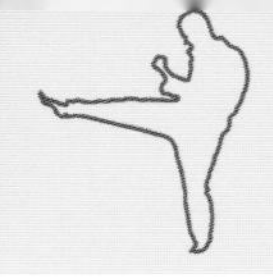

1. A executes an attack with a pistol touching D's chest.
2. D counters by doing a right-handed sweeping block to the inside.
3. D turns the weapon in A's direction and can either do a wrist lock or a disarming action.
4. D pulls it further outwards to the left and disarms A.
5. A punch with the weapon at A's head ends the combination.

1. A executes a knife attack upwards at D's head.
2. D does a left-handed sweeping block downwards and at the same time he executes an open-fingered jab with his right hand at A's eyes.
3. D grabs the ball of the thumb from underneath with his right hand and opens A's grip.

4-5. D takes the knife out of A's hand with his left hand.

6. D places his left leg to the rear...
7. ...and ends the combination with semi-circular roundhouse kick at A's head or a shinbone kick at his thigh.

7.1.2 Defense techniques blocking with the foot (Ashi-waza)

- The defense is done as chosen with the sole of the foot, outside edge of the foot or the ball of the foot against attacks that have at least been started.

1

2

3

1. A makes the start of a kick sideways.
   D preempts him and executes a left-legged stopping kick at the height of the knee on the leg, which he is still lifting to make the kick.
2. The left leg is then placed to the rear.
3. This is then followed by executing a right-legged shinbone kick across both knees.

1-2. A executes a kick backwards with his right leg.
3. D delivers a kick at the rear side of the opponent's thigh before A has time to straighten his leg...
4. ...and places the right leg to the rear.
5. After this D delivers a left-legged shinbone kick at the rear of A's thigh...
6-7. ...followed by a punch with his right fist at A's head.

1. A executes a semi-circular kick at D's thigh.
   D stops the opponent's right leg using the sole of the left foot...
2. ...and places the left leg to the rear.
   Then he punches A's head with his left fist...
3. ...followed by a left uppercut at the head.
4. D places the left leg to the rear...
5. ...and ends the combination with a right-legged shinbone kick at the thigh or a right-footed crescent kick at A's head.

7.1.3 Defense techniques blocking with the lower leg (Ashibo-kake-uke)

- By lifting the knee, the angled lower leg is brought in the direction of the attacking leg.
- In the contact phase, the defending leg is used as a bar, that is to say the lower leg cushions the blow by it giving way.
- Either the shinbone or the outside of the leg is used in the defensive technique.

7.1.3.1 Outwards

1. A executes a shinbone kick (Low Kick) at D's left thigh.
2-3. D carries out a left-legged block outwards with his shinbone and at the same time covers the left side of the body with the left arm, as it can be difficult to recognize at what height the kick is aimed.
4. D places his left foot to the rear (feet 90° to A) and...
5. ...executes a right-legged shinbone kick at A's front thigh.
6. Punch with the left fist (cross).

7. Right uppercut to A's chin.

8. D places his right leg next to A's left leg, places his own head on A's right side and grabs him round the upper body with his right arm.

9-12. D throws A with a major outer hip throw down to the ground.

13. D moves into the mounted straddle position...

14. ...brings the right forearm underneath A's neck, grips his own left biceps with the right hand and lays his right hand on A's face and his own head on top of it, pushes with the shoulder against A's chin and applies a neck lock.

1-2. A executes a left-legged shinbone kick (low kick) at the inside of D's left thigh. D carries out a block outwards with his right shinbone...

3. ...followed by a left uppercut.

4. D turns in to the front of A lays his right hand round A's neck...

5. ...bends forward and grabs hold of A's left lower leg (between his legs)...

6. ...and executes a 'Sambo-roll' throw.

7. The attacker is immobilized on the ground by using a stretched leg lock.

1. A executes a right-footed front kick at D's stomach.
2. D carries out a right-legged shinbone block outwards.
3. A is turned as a result of this and stands with his back to D.

4-5. D executes a shinbone kick (low kick) at the rear of the right thigh...

6. ...grabs hold of the head with both hands...

7. ...and jumps round counterclockwise to A and delivers a kick with his left knee at A's head.

8. D leads A's right arm outwards to the right.

9. With a right-legged sweep of the leg he causes A to fall down.

10. With a downwards stamp on A's knee the combination is ended.

7.1.3.2 Inwards

1. A executes a right-legged shinbone kick (low kick) at D's left thigh.
2. D counters with a right-legged shinbone kick inwards. As he does he covers his upper body well with both arms at the same time...
3-5. ...followed by a right-legged sideways kick at the back of A's left knee.

6. After that D does a foot sweep of A's right foot.
7. A is brought to the ground.
8. A kick downwards on A's knee ends the combination.

1. A executes a left-legged shinbone kick at the inside of D's left thigh.
2-3. D counters with a left-legged shinbone block on the left thigh...
4. ...followed by a right-fisted punch at the head...
5. ...and a left uppercut at the head.

6. D moves round to the right side of A's body...

7. ...and brings him to the ground using a backwards bending throw.

8. D gets into the mounted straddle position...

9. ...slips his right knee over A's right forearm...

10. ...places the left foot next to the left side of A's head and locks the right arm over his own thigh.

1. A executes a left-legged shinbone kick at the inside of D's left thigh.

2-3. D counters with a left-legged shinbone block inwards...

4-5. ...and turns clockwise further round (mainly 180°)...

6-7. ...and executes a crescent right-footed kick at A's head...
8. ...and then places the right foot to the rear...
9. ...delivers a left-legged shinbone kick at the inside of A's thigh...
10. ...places his left foot behind A's left heel...
11-12. ...and brings A to the ground using a foot sweep.
13. The combination is ended by carrying out a downwards kick on the ankle.

7.2 Atemi techniques

7.2.1 Elbow techniques (Empi-uchi)

- Delivering a strike with the elbow is done either by bringing it in straight or in a semi-circle onto the target.
- The effect of the technique is increased by putting the weight of the body behind the blow (changing the center of gravity of the body).
- The free hand gives support by either making contact with the opponent or by protecting the body.
- Closing the fists as the technique is executed is not essential.

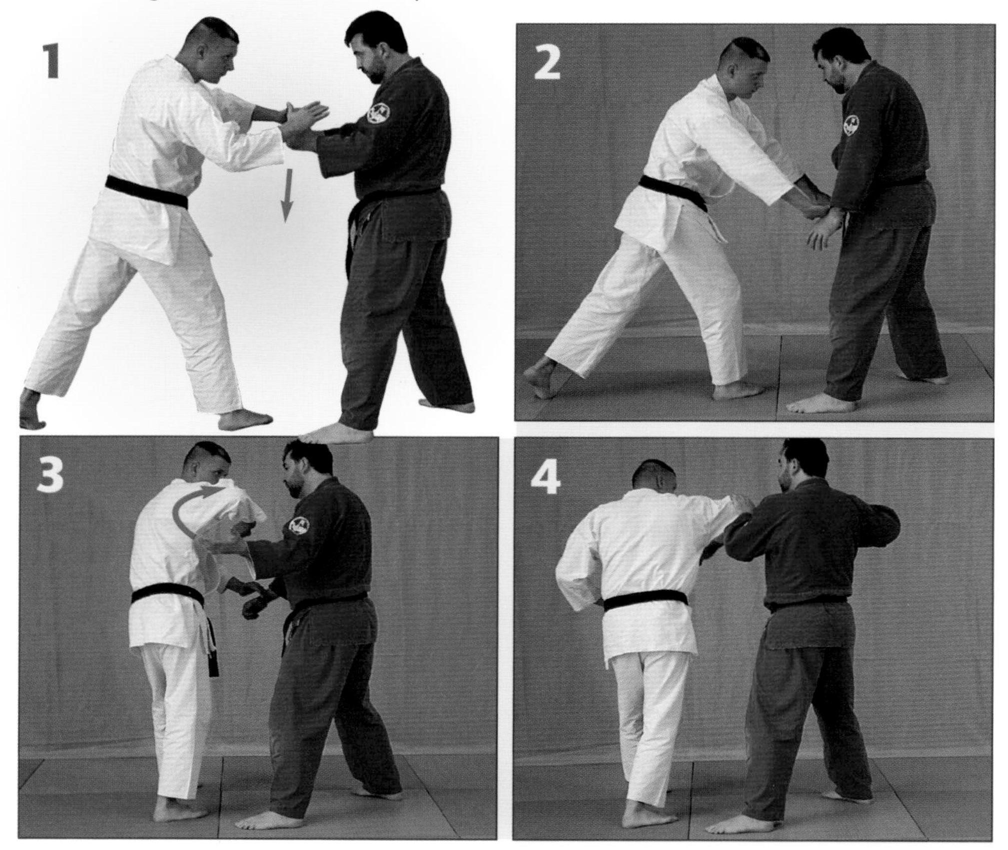

1-2. With both hands, A knocks D's covering hands downwards...
3. ...and moves forward to make an elbow strike at D's head.
4. D sweeps the elbow strike away inwards with his left hand...

5. ...and he now delivers an elbow strike with his right arm forwards to the head.
6. D lifts A's right arm outwards up to A's head...
7. ...and brings A's head downwards in a clockwise direction onto his left elbow.
8-9. D brings A down on to the ground with a twist throw...
10-11. ...and ends the combination with a semi-circular kick with his foot at A's head.

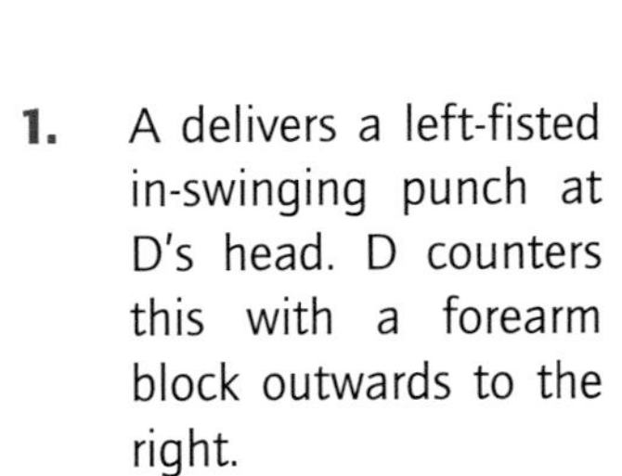

1. A delivers a left-fisted in-swinging punch at D's head. D counters this with a forearm block outwards to the right.
2. A delivers a second swinging punch, this time with the right fist. D counters with a left-handed sweep downwards counterclockwise.
3. D delivers a right elbow strike on the biceps (Sandwich)...
4. ...lifts the arm up a little with his right...
5. ...and delivers an upwards punch at the right liver.
6. Then a right-fisted back-hand punch at A's chin...
7. ...followed by a left-fisted punch at the chin...
8. ...and ends the combination with a semi-circular kick with the right foot at the head or a shinbone kick at the right leg (dependent on agility).

1. A delivers a swinging punch at D's spleen.
D counters with a left forearm block downwards and outwards and with a right hand jab at the neck.

2. With the right arm he brings A's right arm outwards in a counterclockwise direction...

3. ...and with his left he controls the arm about the height of the right elbow.

4. An upward punch is delivered at the liver.

5. The neck is grabbed hold of from round the right side of the head and the head is pulled down on to a knee strike.

6-7. The combination is ended with a left elbow strike onto the backbone.

1. A is holding D's shoulder with his right arm.
2. D counters with a backwards executed left elbow strike at A's head...
3. ...then he brings the left hand over A's head and places this on A's lower back.
4. The right hand grips under the chin.
5. D forces A down to the ground by bending his body over.
6. The left knee is lying on the neck, the right knee is to the side.

   D applies an arm lock on the inside (stretched arm lock) as an immobilization technique.

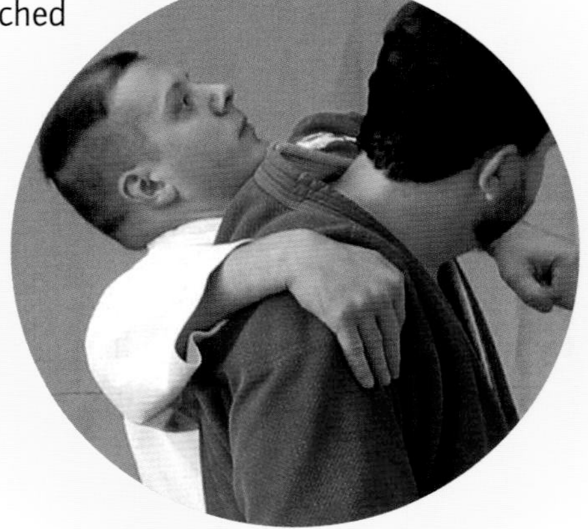

1. A is strangling D from behind with the right forearm.
D takes a step backwards with his right foot, so that he can bend forward and he then grabs hold of A's right wrist with his right hand...

2-3. ...and executes a left elbow strike rearwards at A's stomach...

4. ...followed by a left-handed back of the hand punch at the genitalia...

5. ...and a further backhand punch at the face with the left hand.

6. The right hand frees him from the stranglehold.
D ducks backwards underneath A's arm...

7. ...grabs hold of A's right elbow with his left hand...

8. ...and forces A to the ground using a stretched arm lock.

7.2.2 'Sword hand' techniques (Shuto-uchi)

- Tensed hand, fingers closed, thumb slightly bent.
- The muscular part of the outside edge of the hand strikes the target in a semi-circular (crescent) motion.
- Possible to carry out the technique in any direction.

1. A executes a right-fisted punch at D's head.
2. This is swept away outwards with the right/left (back of the hand).
3-5. A sword hand strike to the neck–right/left/right (scissors).
6. The back of the left hand is brought over A's face and placed on the upper part of A's back.
D grabs between A's legs with his right hand and places the hand on A's back.
7. D lifts A up...
8. ...turns him so that his head is pointing in the direction of the ground...
9. ...and throws him on the ground.

4

5

6

7

8

9

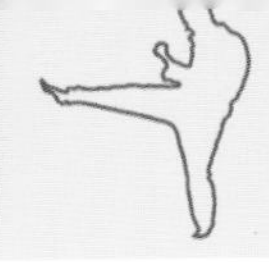

10. D goes down into the crossover position and with his left hand he grabs hold of A's left wrist...

11. ...pushes the right arm through under A's left arm and takes hold of his own left wrist pulls A's arm towards his hips and pushes the elbows up so that the bent arm lock takes proper effect.

1. A executes a knife attack (knife held like an ice-pick) downwards and inwards at D's head.

2. D counters with a left forearm block outwards and at the same time he carries out a sword hand strike with his right hand at A's neck.

3. D grabs hold of A's right wrist with his left hand twists A's wrist with his left hand counterclockwise.
The flat, blunt side of the knife lies on A's left forearm.

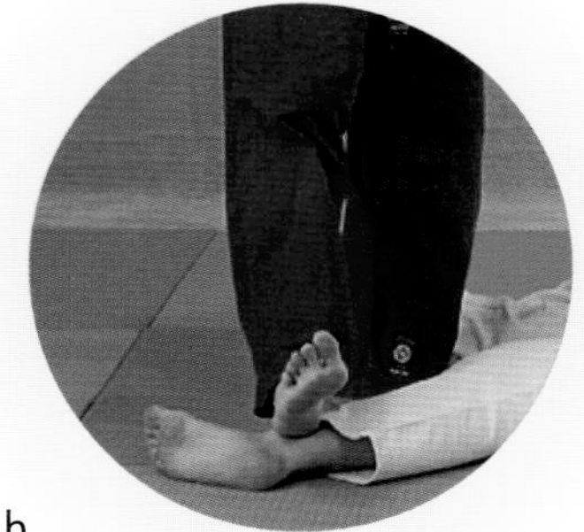

4. With his right hand, D takes hold of the ball of A's thumb...
5. ...and removes the knife from A with his left hand.
6. D places the left foot behind A's right heel...
7-8. ...and throws A to the ground with a foot sweep.
9. A downward kick at the ankle or the knee ends the combination.

1. A executes a strike with a stick downwards onto D's head.
2. D sweeps the arm with the weapon away downwards with his left arm...
3. ...and brings the stick onto A's right shinbone/knee.
4. D delivers a right-handed sword hand strike at A's neck...
5. ...twists the hand holding the weapon upwards more...
6. ...and disarms A with the right forearm, while at the same time the hand carries on to deliver a hand jab into A's eyes.
7. The right arm is brought downwards round A's right arm and a bent arm lock is applied.
   The left hand pushes A's head over to the left side (no image).

7.2.3 Shinbone kicks (Keikotsu-geri, low kick)

- Execution is carried out using the shinbone of the slightly bent leg, which is tensed and locked in that position as the strike lands.
- After making a turn-in about the axis of the body over the standing leg, the leg is brought swinging in onto the target with the supporting impetus of the hips.

1. A executes a right-legged shinbone kick (Low Kick) at D's forward leg. D pulls his leg back so that the attacker's leg misses...

2. ...and takes a step forward with the left foot and executes a right-legged shinbone kick at A's left thigh.

3. From this position, he kicks backwards with the left foot at the genitalia.

4-5. A left-footed sweep forces A to fall down.

6. A right-fisted punch at the head ends the combination.

1. A delivers a right-fisted punch at D's head. D ducks backwards and sweeps the attacking arm inwards with the left arm.
2. D changes his leading leg stance on the spot.
3. This is followed by a left-legged shinbone kick at the inside of the left thigh...
4. ...as well as a right-fisted punch at A's head...
5. ...and an in-swinging left-fisted punch at A's head...
6. ...plus a right uppercut at A's head.
7. D places his left foot to the rear...
8. ...and ends the combination with a right-legged roundhouse kick at the upper body or the head.

1. A executes a right-footed front kick.
   D steers this outwards with his left leg...
2. ...places his left leg to the rear...
3. ...and delivers a right-legged shinbone kick at the inside of the right thigh.
4. The left foot is placed behind A's left foot...
5. ...and using a leg lock, A is forced to the ground.
6. A downward kick at the ankle ends the combination.

7.2.4 Downward kick with the foot (Kakato-geri)

- Knee is pulled up and then brought downwards sharply.
- The striking surfaces can be the heel or the outside edge of the foot.

1. A executes a right-legged shinbone kick at the outside of D's left thigh.
2. At the same time as the attack, D takes a step to the right with his right leg and delivers a shinbone kick with his left leg at the inside of A's left thigh.
3. D grabs hold of the head round the right-hand side of A's head...
4. ...and pulls the head down and delivers a kick at A's head with his right foot...

5-6. ...bringing A down with left-legged sweep of the foot...

7. ...and ends the combination with a downward kick at A's knee or ankle.

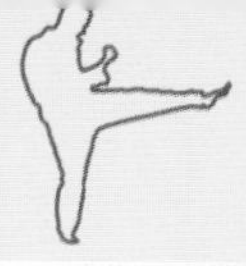

1. A grabs hold of D's diametrically opposed wrist.

2. D counters with a left-fisted punch coming in on A's right elbow (breaking the grip)...

3. ...followed by a right-handed palm heel strike at A's genitalia.

4-5. D stands behind A and grabs hold of A's groins with the middle fingers of both hands and pulls back hard to the rear and downwards (45°).

6-7. A downward kick at A's upper body ends the combination.

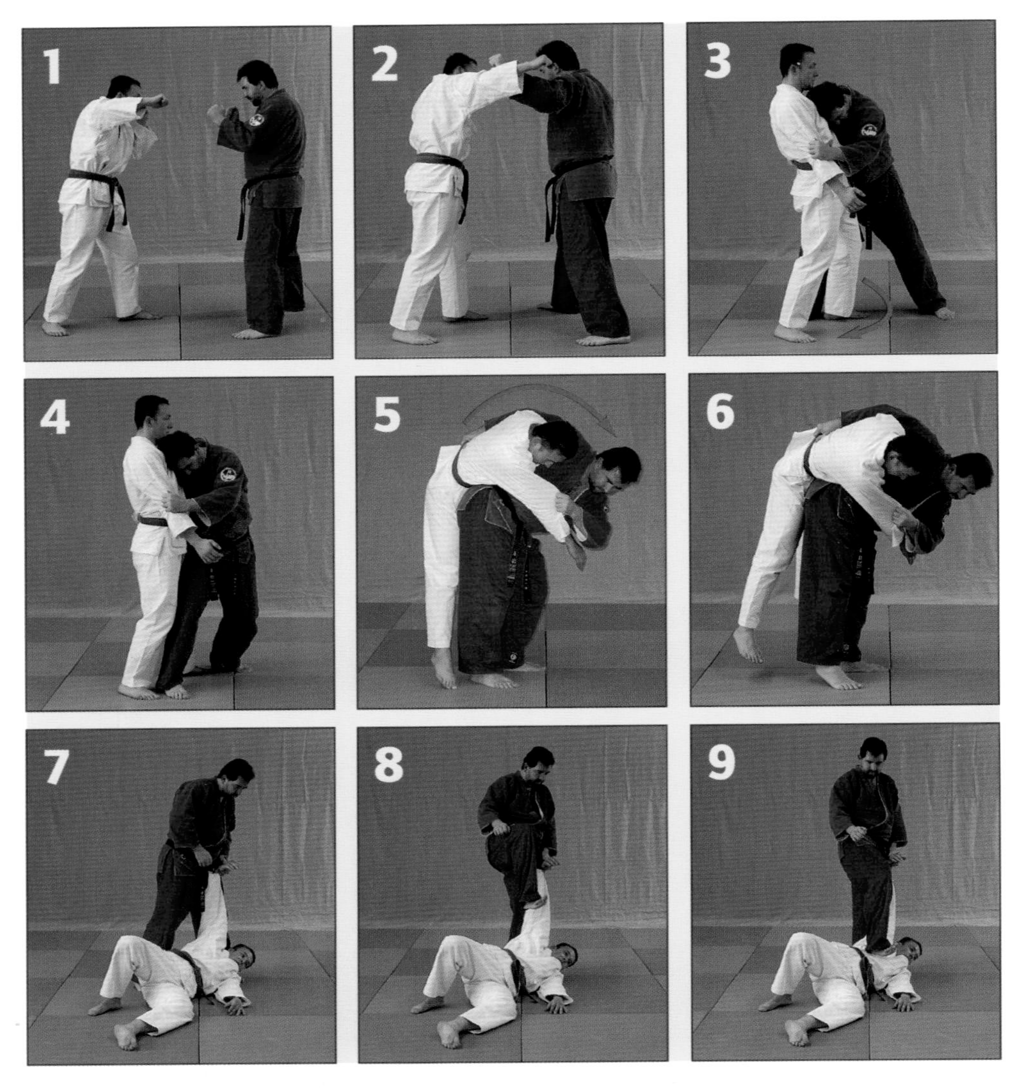

1. A delivers an in-swinging right-fisted punch at D's head.
2. D counters with a left forearm block outwards.
Keeping his cover up protecting his head he goes forward to the right.
D's right arm lies over A's left arm.
D is standing at 90° to A.
The left hand is holding A's right arm.
4. D pushes his hips forwards in front of A...
5-7. ...and throws him with a major outer hip throw to the ground.
8-9. A downward kick ends the combination.

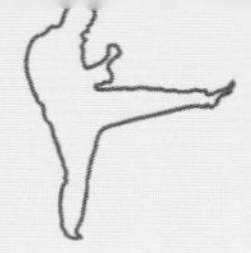

7.2.5 Sideways kick (Yoko-geri)

- Lift the knee while looking sideways at the attacker.
- Stretch the leg and the hips in the direction of the target, followed by a withdrawing kick movement.
- The striking surface is the tensed outside edge of the foot or the heel.
- Carried out at least horizontally or higher.

1. A executes a right-legged front kick at D's stomach.
   D takes a lunge step to the left with his left foot and at the same time counters with a forearm block downwards and outwards to the right against the attacking leg.
2. A turns through the block so that he is standing with his back to D afterwards.
3. D pulls the right knee in to the hips...
4. ...and delivers a sideways kick at A's back.

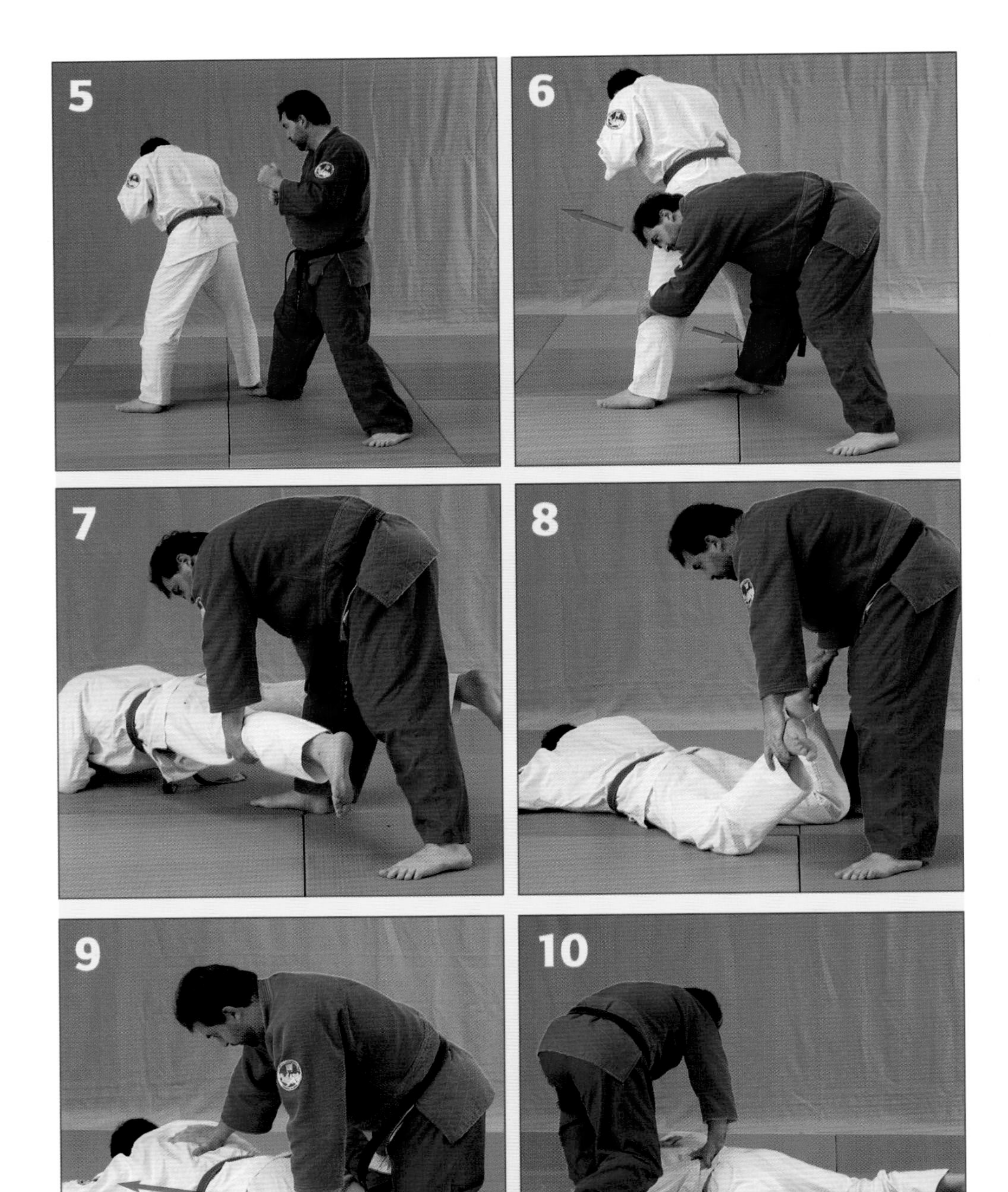
5
6
7
8
9
10

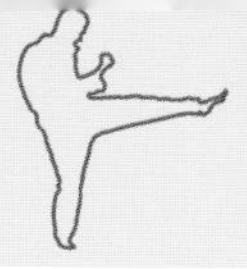

5. D places the **right** leg forward...
6. ...grabs round A's thighs...
7-8. ...and forces A to fall down forward using a double hand sweep.
9. D climbs over A's right leg with his right leg and applies a bent leg lock.
10. D moves to get diagonally over A's back (before this he instructs A to put his left arm on his back)...
11. ...and applies a crossover grip (bent arm lock).
12. Using this he can then move A about.

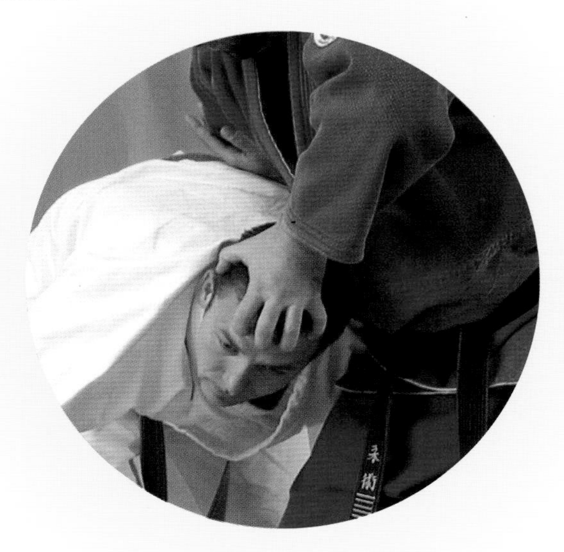

1. A starts to apply a grip on D's neck with both hands.

2. D counters with a sideways kick at A's stomach.

3. D grabs hold of A with his right hand on A's neck and his left hand on the chin.

4. D brings the head underneath his left armpit, placing the back of his own right hand directly under the armpit...

5. ...swings the forearm round the neck grabs hold of his own right wrist with his left hand, brings his knees together (crossed) to protect the genitalia and stretches himself up so that the neck lock becomes effective.

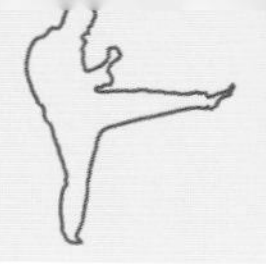

1. A executes a roundhouse kick at D's upper body.
D dodges back...

2. ...and sweeps the attacking leg outwards to the right with his right arm.

3. D pulls the right knee up to the chest...

4. ...and delivers a sideways kick at A's back.

5. D places the right leg forwards and grabs hold of A's head.

6-7. By pulling on the head at the same time as executing a sweeping right-legged foot kick at A's left leg, he forces A to fall down.

8-9. A circular left-footed kick at A's head ends the combination.

7.3 Applying pressure to nerve points

- Pressure applied to all available vital areas that react to pain of this sort.

1. A is executing a frontal bear hug under the arms.
2. D places the thumbs of both of his hands in the hollows below A's ears.
3. D grabs hold of A, with his left hand on A's neck and with his right hand on the chin and pushes A's head down into his neck.

4-5. Using a twisting neck hold, D forces A to the ground.

6. With an inside arm lock (stretched arm lock) D immobilizes A on the ground. To do this he places his left knee on the side of the neck and the right knee on the side of the upper body near A's hips.

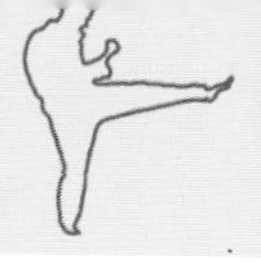

1. A grabs hold of D's collar from behind.
2. D turns round to A. The left hand grabs hold of the neck. The inside edge of the right hand is held under the nose.
3. By applying pressure against the nose and downwards, A is forced to the ground.
4. D climbs over A's head with his left leg and places it down.
5. D lays the right foot over A's right outstretched arm and places the knee on the ground and applies a stretched arm lock to immobilize him.

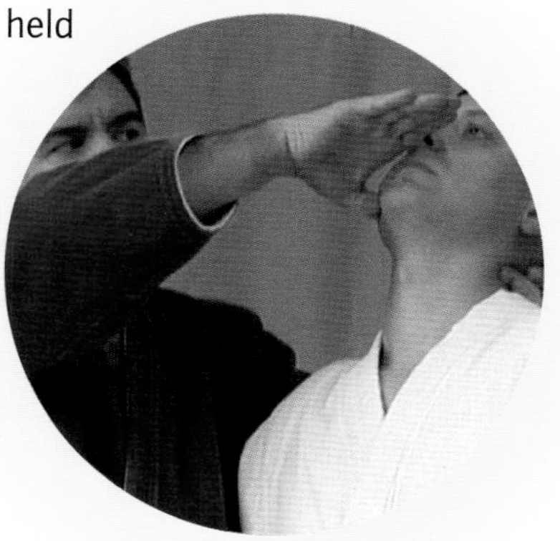

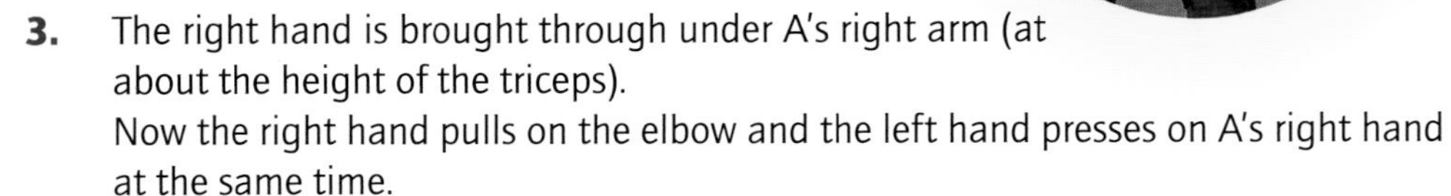

1. A is strangling D frontally with both hands.
2. D presses into the hollow of the larynx (pressure point) until A loosens his grip.
   As he does this D holds A's right hand firm with his left hand.
3. The right hand is brought through under A's right arm (at about the height of the triceps).
   Now the right hand pulls on the elbow and the left hand presses on A's right hand at the same time.
4. The left hand is placed on the rear side of the right upper arm (near to the elbow).
5. The hips are pushed in front of A's shoulders.
   The right hand grips into the eye sockets and pulls the head back at the neck.
   With a crossed grip (bent arm lock for transporting) A can now be moved about.

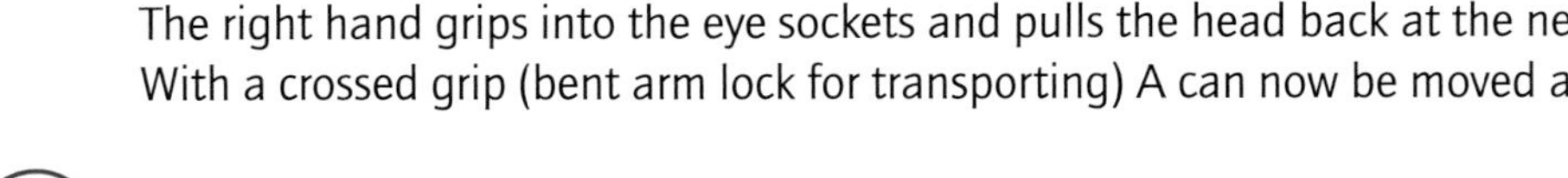

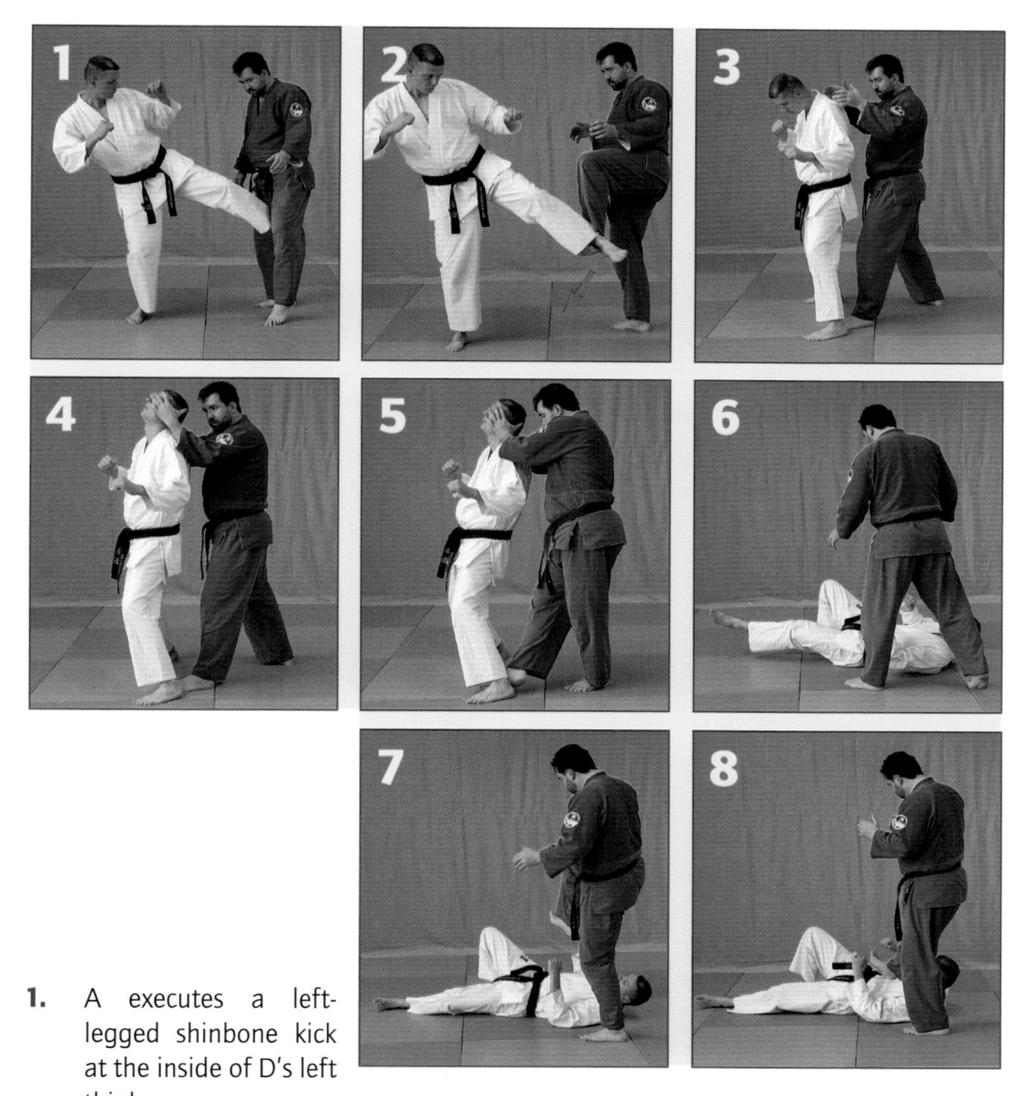

1. A executes a left-legged shinbone kick at the inside of D's left thigh.
2. D lifts the left leg up...
3. ...lets A's leg go past and then brings his left leg inwards to protect his genitalia, D places (shoves) the left leg directly behind A's left thigh.
4. D grabs A's eyes with the middle fingers (pressure on the nerve) and at the same time presses A 's ears with his thumbs so that A cannot dodge away.

5-6. Now D makes a step turn backwards, clockwise to the left and forces A to fall over by using a pulling, bending movement combined with a sweep of the right foot.

7-8. D ends the combination with a downward kick.

7.4 Stranglehold techniques

7.4.1 Stranglehold techniques with the arms or hands (Jime-waza)

- Any form of strangling technique executed by the hands or the arms.
- The effect of the technique is achieved by disrupting the circulation of blood to the brain as well as the flow of air to the lungs.

1

1. A executes a left-legged shinbone kick (low-kick) at the inside of D's thigh. D lifts his left leg up and inwards over A's attacking leg.
2. D places it directly behind A's left leg...
3. ...and pushes forwards left so that A turns and stands with his back to D.

4. D grabs round A's body...

5. ...lifts him up about 20 cm...

6. ...and let's him drop slightly into his knees...

7. ...and takes him down with him on to the ground lying on his back grabs A's left arm with his left hand near the wrist bringing both of his feet over A's thighs. D brings his right arm round in front of A's neck and places his right hand on A's left shoulder...

8. ...and then D pushes his left hand behind A's head (the back of the hand is placed behind the head) pulls the shoulder blades together and applies a stranglehold on A ("Mata Leao").

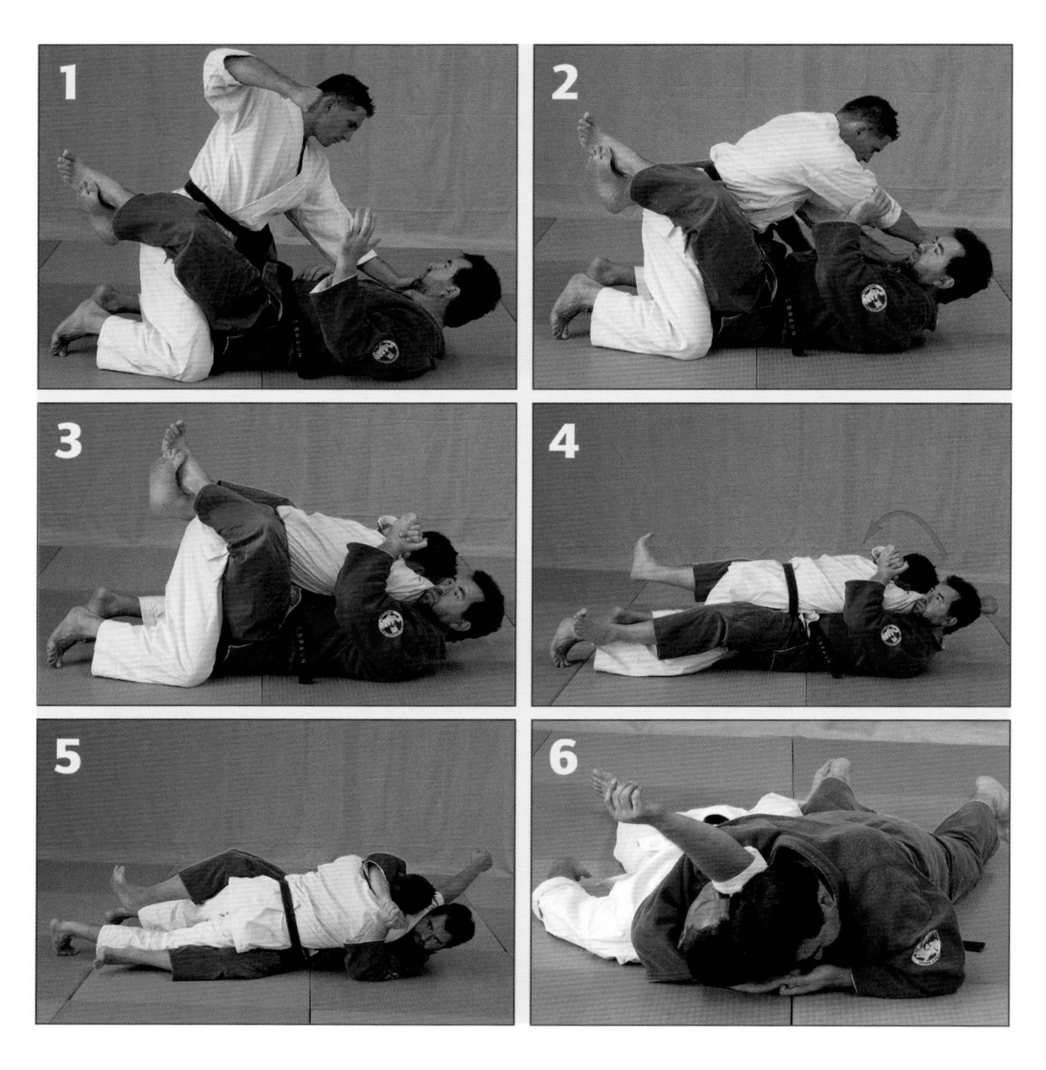

1. A is between D's legs in the 'Guard' position and delivers a punch at D's head. D has clamped his legs round A's body.
2. D pulls his legs up and sweeps the attacking arm with his left inwards...
3. ...grabs hold round A's neck with his right hand (A's arms are now pinned in) takes hold of his own right wrist with his left hand...
4. ...and by stretching his legs hard (near to the ground) causes A to lie down from the kneeling position D pins both legs with his own legs...

5-6. ...turns him over onto his back lies down directly next to the right side of A's body. D's head is directly next to A's right shoulder.
By pulling in the arms, a stranglehold technique with the hands/arms is effected.

1-2. A executes a stick strike from the right inside to the middle of D's body. D counters with a right-handed sweep from the outside to the inside and at the same time takes a step backwards with his left foot.

3. D executes a right-handed finger jab (disrupting action) at A's eyes.

4. The right hand grabs hold of the ball of A's right thumb.

5. D brings the weapon carrying hand outwards again

6. D lifts his left leg up and pulls the hand bearing the weapon hard over his left thigh...

7. ...and carries out a disarming movement.

8. The right hand takes hold of the larynx and the left hand is placed in the back...

9. ...and A is forced to the ground using the stranglehold on the larynx and immobilized.

7.4.2 Stranglehold techniques using clothing (Jime-waza)

- Any stranglehold that is carried out by using the defender's or the opponent's clothing.
- The effect of the technique is achieved by disrupting the circulation of blood to the brain as well as the flow of air to the lungs.

1. A executes a stick attack from the right downward and inwards at D's head.
2. D counters with a right-arm shoulder stop and covers his own face with his left hand.
3. D brings (sweep of the hand) the hand holding the weapon downwards and outwards with his right hand and at the same time delivers a left-handed finger jab at A's eyes (no image).

4. D changes over to controlling the hand with the weapon by using his left hand and gripping the ball of the thumb.
5. He disarms A using the right forearm and delivers a finger jab at A's right eye as he does this.
6. D rolls the right arm over A's right arm...
7. ...and lays his right hand on the right of A's chest moving behind him as he does this.
8. D grabs hold of A's left lapel with his right hand and grabs deep into A's collar round his neck with his left hand.
9. D executes a right-footed kick at the hollow at the back of A's right knee and by pulling on both the lapel and the collar he applies a stranglehold on A.

1. A is sitting in the mounted position on top of D.
2. D delivers a right-fisted punch at A's genitals.
3. Because of this, A comes downwards a little.
4. D grips the right hand side of A's collar with his right-hand thumb...
5. ...and with his left-hand thumb he grips the left hand side of A's collar and applies a crossover stranglehold with the clothing.
5. As he does this, D tries to get his elbow on to the ground and pull A downwards.

1. A grabs hold of D's diagonally opposed right wrist.
2. D twists his right arm clockwise upwards breaks the grip with his left arm striking A's right arm from the outer side.
3. D brings his right arm round A's neck and moves round behind A.
4. The knuckles of the left hand are pressed against the left side of A's neck and the right hand grabs hold of the sleeve of his own left forearm. By pulling on his sleeve and pressing with the knuckles of the left hand against the vein in the neck the stranglehold is brought into effect.

7.5 Levering techniques–Locks

7.5.1 Wrist locks

1. A executes an attack with the stick coming inwards at the legs.
2. D counters by using a right-handed sweep outwards and at the same time with a left-handed jab at the eyes.
3. D places the left hand underneath A's right elbow and delivers a further right-handed jab at the eyes...
4. ...and, with his right hand he then grabs hold of the ball of the thumb of the hand holding the weapon...
5. ...brings the arm in the direction of A's body and smacks the stick on the legs.

6. D brings the stick further round behind A places the stick on A's back in the area of his kidneys and pulls A's right hand along close to his upper body.
7. Thus, A is disarmed using the body.
8. D reaches over A's right arm with his left arm and grabs hold of his own right wrist and throws A with a bent arm lock backwards. When the bent arm lock has been carried out, D can strike at A's head with his elbow.
9. A bent hand lock immobilizes A on the ground.

1. A grabs hold of the opposing sleeve with his left hand.
2. D lifts the right arm up until the little finger of A's left hand is pointing upwards.
3. D brings A's left hand (that is slightly bent forward) up to A's right shoulder.
4. By applying pressure with the shoulder forwards the side twisting hand lock is increased.

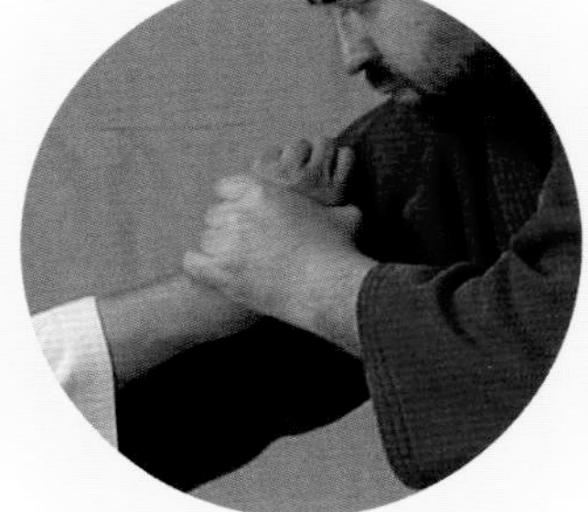

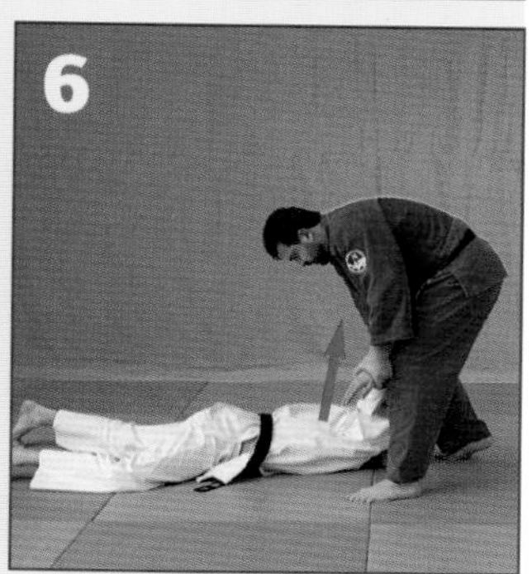

1. A grabs hold of D's diagonally opposed wrist.
2. D turns his body round further clockwise and grabs hold of A's right wrist with his left hand.
   D places A's right arm on the side of his left upper body.
3. D levers the right arm over the side of the body and forces A to move forward.
4. D executes a sharp twist in the other direction...
5. ...and throws A down to the ground with a bent hand lock in combination with a step turn.
   D places the right hand on the elbow...
6. ...and turns A over on to his stomach.
7. D grabs hold of A's right wrist with his right hand...
8. ...and can then transport A with a bent hand lock.

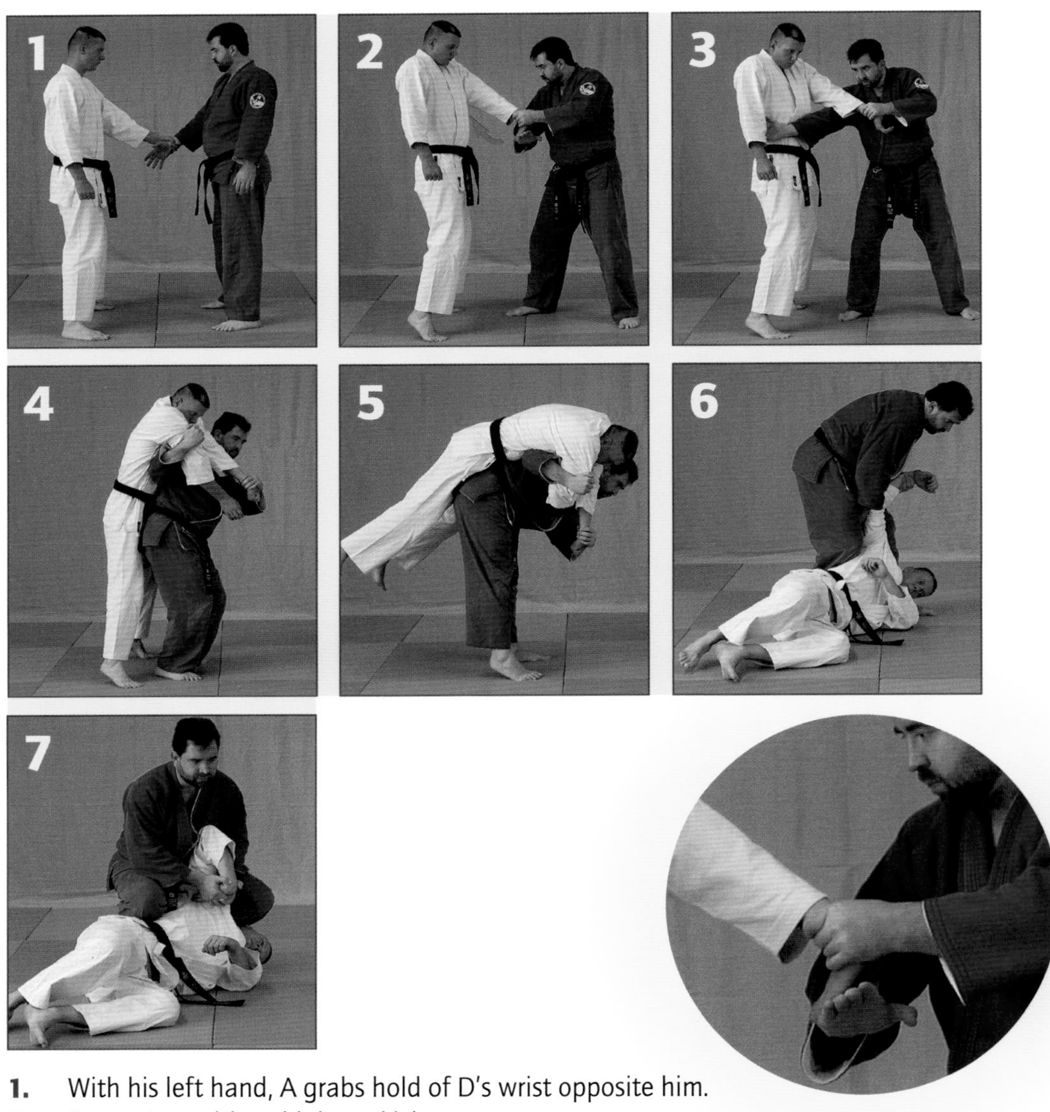

1. With his left hand, A grabs hold of D's wrist opposite him.
2. D counters with a shinbone kick.
   The left hand grabs hold of A's left wrist.
   With his right hand, D presses against A's right hand and executes a locking hand block.
3. D brings his right arm through underneath A's right arm...
4. ...throws A with a shoulder throw...

5-6. ...onto the ground.

7. D immobilizes A on the ground with a bent hand lock.

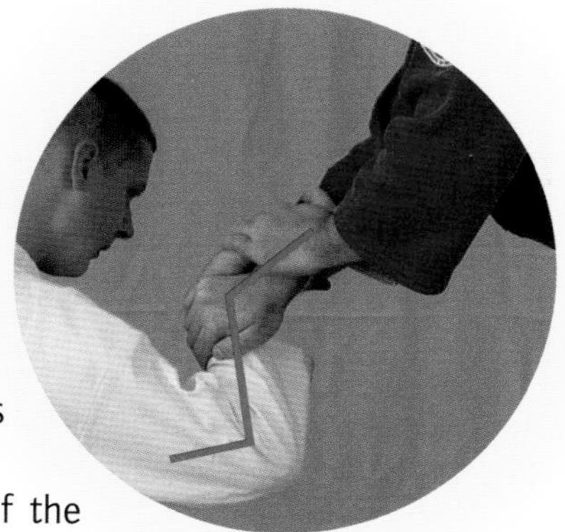

1. A grabs hold of D's diagonally opposed wrist.
2. D counters with a shinbone kick and takes hold of A's right hand at the same time with his left hand.
3. D executes a clockwise twisting movement of the hand and grabs hold of A's right wrist.
4. D now brings A's hand as near as possible in to A's solar plexus, so that A's arm takes the form of a 'Z'.
5. In this position, D pushes A's arm with a twisting hand lock downwards, ensuring that the form of the 'Z' is maintained. The hips are pulled back away so that A cannot easily attack the genital area.

7.5.2 Transporting techniques using the bent arm lock (Ude-garami)

- Any extension applied on the opponent's bent arm having an effect on the elbow and/or the shoulder joint.
- The technique must be made so that the opponent can be moved about.

1. A executes a strike with a stick coming horizontally inwards from outside right at D's hips.
2. D sweeps the arm holding the weapon diagonally downwards and outwards with his right arm simultaneously delivering a finger jab at the eyes (disrupting action).
3. The left hand takes over the job of holding the right wrist (checking the arm holding the weapon)...
4. ...and the right hand levers the stick with a forearm motion out of A's right hand.
5. In the same movement, a right-handed finger jab at the eyes is delivered.
6. D brings his right arm in a circular motion outwards, downwards and then inwards and grips into the crease of A's right elbow with the middle finger of the right hand...

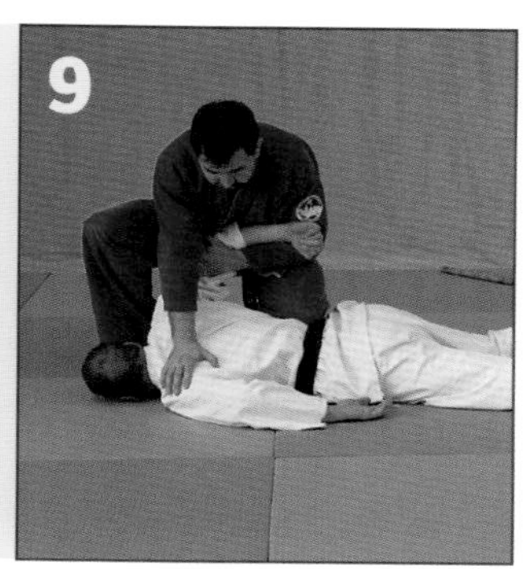

7. ...and forces A down on the ground with a bent arm lock.
D places his right hand on A's right elbow...

8. ...and turns him over on to his stomach.

9. D places the right hand on A's right elbow, holding on to the left shoulder with his right hand as he does this so that A cannot turn himself round...

10. ...and by lifting with his own left arm makes A stand up, while changing over to holding A's head with his right hand and pulls it into the neck.
With a crossed over grip (bent arm lock as a 'transporting lever') he moves A along.

1. A grabs hold of D's left lapel with his right hand and delivers a left-fisted punch (in-swinging hook) at D's head.
2. D counters by doing a right forearm block outwards to the right. At the same time, the left hand pins A's right hand to his own upper body.
3. D delivers a punch at the solar plexus.
4. D's right hand grabs hold of A's upper arm from behind...
5. ...and pulls this forward, pushing the forearm backwards to the rear at the same time.
6. D grabs hold of A's right upper arm with his left hand near to the elbow...
7. ...and ends the combination with a crossed over grip (bent arm lock 'transporting lever').

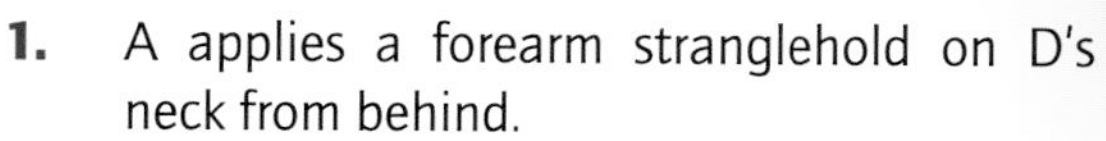

1. A applies a forearm stranglehold on D's neck from behind.
2. D delivers a jab with his left thumb at A's left eye.
3. D frees himself from the stranglehold...
4. ...and moves from under A's arm to the rear...
5. ...bringing and twisting A's right arm up behind his back in a bent arm lock grasps with his left hand into A's eyes from above and moves A along with the bent arm lock in combination with pressure on the eyes (gouging the nerve point).

7.5.3 Stretched arm lock (Ude-gatame)

- Extension of the opponent's elbow joint by pulling the wrist and exerting pressure on the elbow joint.
- The defender applies the levered lock on the opponent as he lies on the ground.
- Possible ways of carrying out the lever hold: Any type of arm lock that can be chosen.
- The techniques carried out when standing and when the opponent is on the ground can be identical (i.e., both can be with a stretched arm lever over the thigh/groin)

Execution in the standing position

1. A executes a strike with a stick coming in from up to the right downwards to the head.
2. Using the three-step contact, D brings the attacking arm inwards:
   Left forearm block outwards.
   The right hand is brought up under A's right arm.
3. Using a sweeping motion (like a windscreen wiper) with the right arm, A's right arm is brought out to the right...

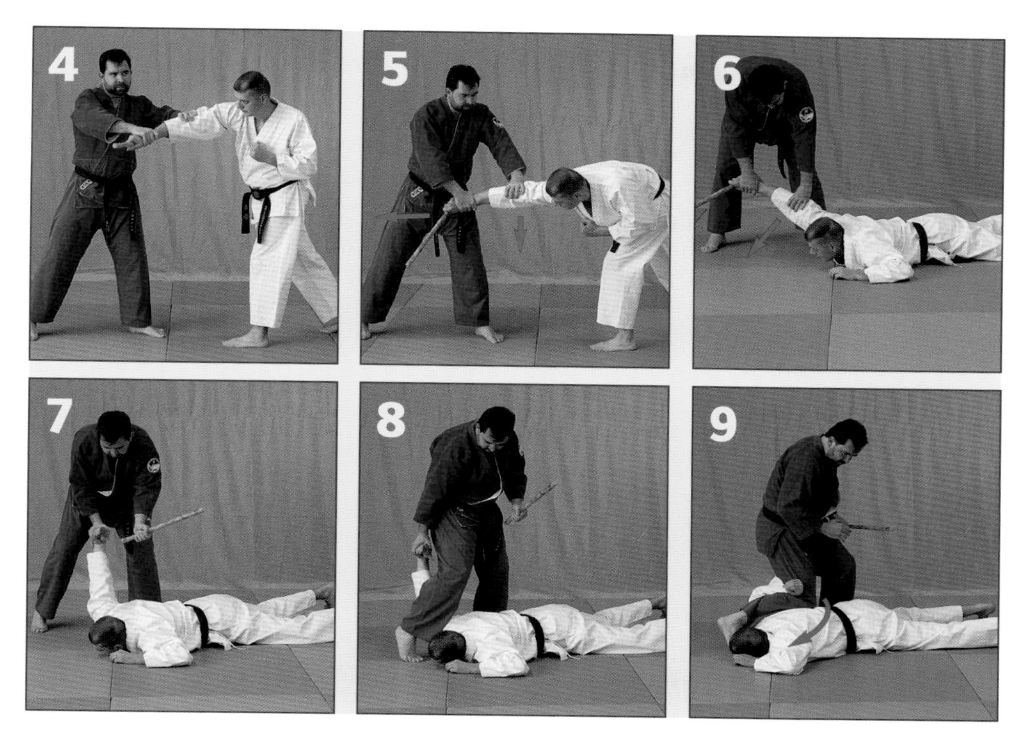

4. ...and the right elbow joint is held pinned by the left hand. The right hand grabs A's right wrist.

5. By pulling the wrist, the arm is stretched and pressure applied to the elbow and a stretched arm lock is applied while standing.

6-7. D brings A down on to the ground using the lock...

8. ...places his right leg over A's right arm...

9. ...and wraps the right arm round his right leg and ends the combination by applying a crossed over lock with the leg immobilizing the opponent.

1. A grabs D by both lapels.
2. D delivers a right-fisted punch at A's stomach and, at the same time grabs hold of A's right wrist with his left hand.
3. D slides his left elbow over A's right arm also grabbing A's right wrist with his right hand...
4. ...and then takes a small step to the right creating pressure downwards onto A's elbow with his left arm and carries out a body lock (stretched arm lock).

1. A executes a strike with a stick coming in from up from the left inwards to D's head.
2. With his left hand D brings (sweeping motion) the hand with the weapon in a clockwise direction downwards and outwards to the left and executes a right-handed jab with the fingers at the eyes at the same time...
3. ...with a twisting arm lock (stretched arm lock).
4. D pulls A down to the ground in a straight line...
5. ...and disarms him with his right hand and immobilizes the attacker on the ground with a twisting arm lock (stretched arm lock).

1. A grabs hold of D's diagonally opposed wrist.
2. D counters with a left-footed kick at the right shinbone.
3. D brings his own leg further over to the right and places it down at an angle of 90° to A. D also brings A's right arm forwards and downwards...
4. ...and, in a further movement, brings the right arm over his own left shoulder with a steady pull and applies a stretched arm lock over his own shoulder.
5. D, then, turns clockwise round further...
6. ...and brings A down to the ground with a 'sword' throw.

7-8. D pulls A's right wrist upwards and places his right hand on A's elbow.

9. By pulling on the hand and applying pressure on the elbow, he immobilizes A with this stretched arm lock.

1. A executes a knife attack coming in from up from the left inwards to D's neck.
2. D counters blocking the attack with the back of the left hand at the same time delivering a right-handed jab with the fingers at A's eyes.
3. With a sweeping motion D brings the hand with the weapon in a clockwise direction outwards to the left and takes a step forwards with the right foot and checks A with a reverse body lock (stretched arm lock).
4. D takes the knife from A with his right hand...
5. ...makes a step turn about 180° backwards and traps A's hand using a twisting bent hand lock.
6. D places the pommel of the knife near to A's right elbow...
7. ...and brings A down on to the ground with a stretched arm lock.

Execution on the ground

1. A pushes D down towards the ground and applies a stranglehold with both hands. A is positioned between D's legs, who replies by clamping his legs round A in the region of the kidneys.
2. D delivers a jab with the fingers of the right hand at A's head, while pinning A's right forearm against his own body with his right arm.
3. D brings A's right arm round to the left side of his body (in the direction of the groin) and immobilizes the arm with the right hand. D grabs hold of A's head with his left hand (round the neck from the right side of the head so that A cannot stand up).

4-5. D now rolls his left hand round A's head and pushes it to the left side.

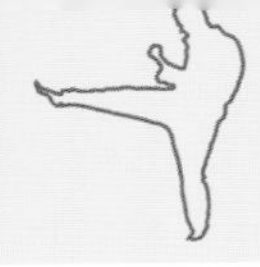

6. D turns his body over about 90° to the right on the ground swings his left leg over A's head, brings his right leg very close to A's left arm i.e., the left leg is lying on A's back and the hollow of his own knee is positioned next to A's left arm. D pulls both of his feet back and pushes his heels on to the ground.

7. Now, D's left hand takes over the immobilization of A's forearm:

- A's right arm is stretched and the left arm is pinned against D's upper body. This is because, by using the forearm, more power can be exerted this way than when the arm is held by the hand.
- D grabs round A's left thigh with the right hand.
- By stretching the hips, a side-stretch lever (stretched arm lock) is applied.

1. A executes a bear hug pinning D's arms down.
2. After D has delivered a stamping thrust on A's left foot in order to give him a shock,
3. he pushes on A's pelvis bones with both arms to get some space between himself and A.
4. After this, D delivers a knee-kick at A's genitalia.
5. D's left hand wraps itself clockwise round A's right arm and holds on round the elbow joint. D's left hand is placed on the right hand and a stretched arm lock (standing) is applied.

6-7. D swings his left leg over A's head and he executes a sling throw.
8. He then conducts a right-footed stamp on A's lower ribcage...
9. ...places his foot forwards over A and turns him onto his stomach...
10. ...ending the combination with an arm lock over the groin.

1. A pushes D in the direction of the ground and delivers a right-fisted punch at D's head. A is positioned between D's legs. D has A under control by applying a scissors-leg clinch round the area of the kidneys.
2. By pulling up on his legs, D brings A forwards off-balance and sweeps the attacking arm to the right with the left hand.
3. D is holding A's right arm
4. and pushes his left foot under A's head. By pushing the hips forward and clamping the arm between the legs while lifting the arms towards the ceiling (with the little finger pointing upwards) a twisting lever (stretched arm lock) is applied.

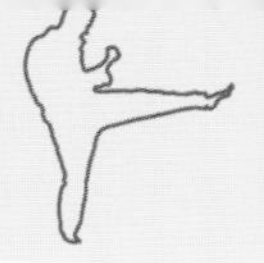

1. A executes a headlock from a side position.
2. D gouges into A's right eye with his left thumb.
   A lets go of his grip and stands upright.
3. D executes a backwards roll so that A falls backward.
4. D moves straight away into the scarf hold (holding position in a sideways stance–also called a *Kesa-gatame*)...
5. ...presses his left hand onto the ground close to A's neck...
6. ...swings his left leg over A's head...
7. ...and applies a side-stretch lock (stretched arm lock).

1. A applies a frontal headlock on D.
2. D delivers a hand jab at A's neck...
3. ...and frees himself from the headlock with the left arm and pulls his head away grabbing between A's legs with his right arm holding on to his bottom/lower back.
   The left hand is placed diagonally over the right neck side on to A's back.
4. D lifts A up by stretching up from his knees turns him into the horizontal position...

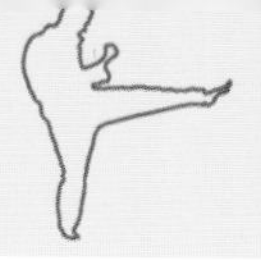

5. ...and lets him drop...
6. ...and goes down on top of him in the straddle position...
7. ...sliding the right knee up over A's left upper arm...
8. ...placing his left foot next to A's ear (the heel is pointing at the neck) and applies a stretched arm lock over the groin to immobilize the opponent.

7.6 Throwing techniques

7.6.1 Shoulder throw (Seoi-nage) or shoulder turn (Seoi-otoshi)

- The opponent can be got hold of in any manner.
- The balance is broken forwards by pulling or by using an Atemi technique.
- Shoulder throw: From the parallel stance, turn in—taking care not to get off-balance—gather up the opponent, following on by lifting, stretching the legs up straight as well as turning the upper body, or by throwing, in that the center of balance is dropped quite low as the opponent is pulled over the shoulder.
- Shoulder turn: Turn in, placing the leg nearest to the opponent out to the side; by turning the body in the opposite direction about the central axis of the body, the opponent is brought with a swing down to the ground.

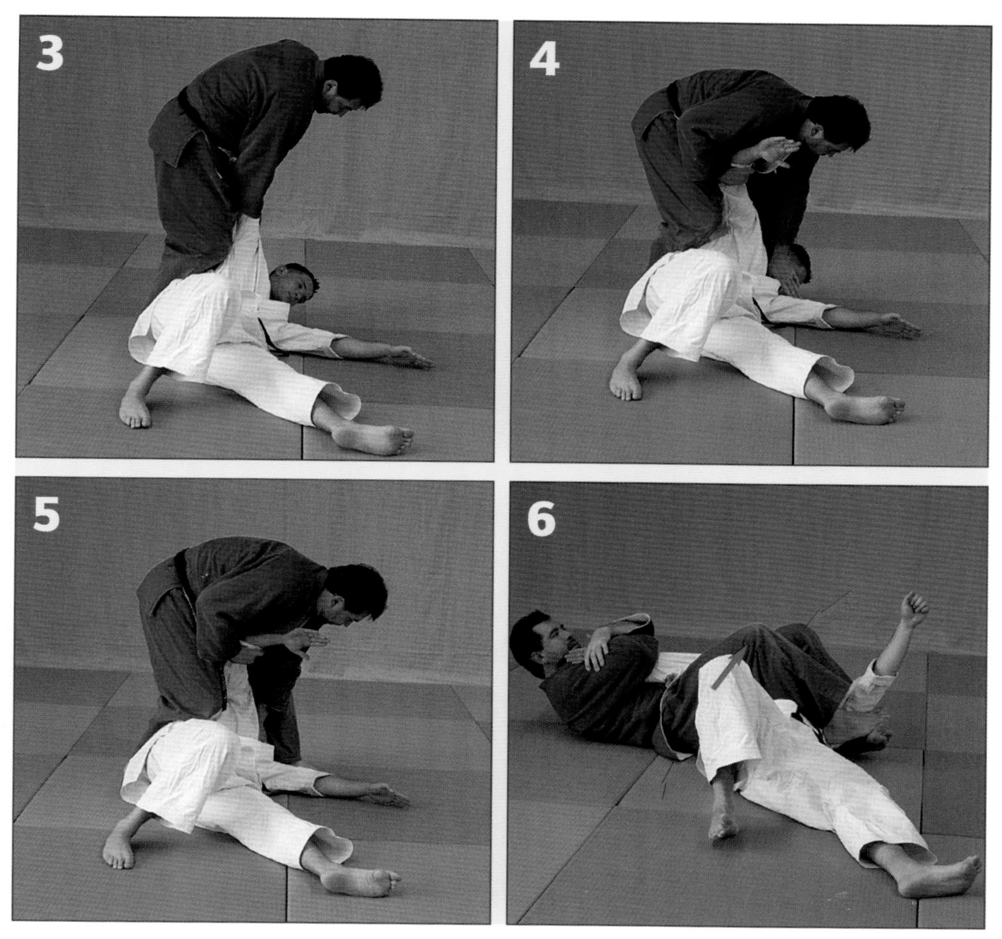

1. A pushes D frontally with both hands.

2-3. D counters by going straight into a shoulder throw (Picture A/Shoulder turn = Picture B)...

4-5. ...and climbs with both legs over A (first the left then the right)...

6. ...and ends the combination with a side-stretch lock (stretched arm lock).

1. A executes a bear hug from behind with both arms trapping D's arms.

2. D counters with a stamping kick on the foot...

3-5. ...and throws A with a shoulder throw (Picture A/Shoulder turn = Picture B) onto the ground.

6. D delivers a right-footed kick at A's ribcage...

7. ...places the leg over A and turns A on to his stomach.
The combination is ended by applying a stretched arm lock over the groin.

1. A has D in a stranglehold from the side.
2. D spreads his shoulders out to make the stranglehold difficult for A to achieve and counters with a sideways elbow strike.
3. D throws A with a shoulder throw (Picture A/Shoulder throw = Picture B) on to the ground.
4. D grabs hold of A's right wrist and places the left hand on the elbow.
5. D turns A over on to his stomach
6.-7 and immobilizes him using a crossed over lock (bent arm lock) with the leg.

7.6.2 Major Inner reaping throw (O-uchi-gari)

- The opponent is put off-balance by pulling and/or pushing him; that is to say Atemi techniques to the side and to the rear by the defender standing in front of him. When executing the throw forwards the above applies in a position behind the attacker.
- By sweeping away the opponent's standing leg using the nearest defender's leg the opponent falls (is thrown) over backwards sideways; when done from behind a leg is caught hold of and swept above the knee in which case the opponent will fall (be thrown) over forwards.
- The defender may optionally follow the opponent down to the ground and control him further on the ground.
- The type of grip to be used is open to the defender.

1. A executes a semi-circular kick with his right foot at D's waist. D catches A's right leg holding it underneath with his left hand...
2. ...and counters with a sword edge strike with his right hand at the right side of A's neck...

3-5. ...and carries out a major inner reaping throw.

6. He then carries out a leg lock on A's right leg.

7-8. D turns A over on to his stomach and applies a spine lock to immobilize him.

1. A delivers a left-fisted punch (in-swinger) at D's head. D counters with a forearm block outwards to the right.
2. A delivers a further right-fisted punch (in-swinger). D counters with a left forearm block outwards...
3. ...followed by a sword hand strike with the right at the right side of the neck.

4-5. D throws A with a major inner reaping throw...
6. ...follows him down to the ground and kneels down over A's right arm, while at the same time applying a right stretched arm lock.
7. He then delivers a sword hand strike at the neck with his right hand.
8. Then D presses A's right arm over his face...
9-10. ...and stands facing A.

1. A delivers a clip of the ear at D's head with his right hand.
2. D sweeps the hand inwards with his right hand...
3. ...takes over holding the attacking hand with his left hand...
4. ...and delivers a sword hand strike with his right hand at the neck.
5-6. D throws A with a major inner reaping throw down to the ground.
7. He then kneels down over the left leg.

8. Lead up to the cross position: His own left leg is crossed over to the right and outside...
9. ...the left leg is then pushed under the right leg.
10. A's right wrist is grabbed hold of with the right hand...
11. ...and with the left hand D reaches through under A's right arm and takes hold of his own right wrist. His own wrist is bent upwards, A's right elbow is brought to his right hip, the right hand is pinned to the ground
12. and A's right upper arm is pressed upwards (bent arm lock as an immobilization technique).

7.6.3 Lifting throws (Ushiro-goshi, Aiki-otoshi, Kata-guruma)

- The opponent is made to lose his balance (center of gravity).
- The lift comes from the action of stretching the legs and pushing the hips forward.
- Where applicable the attacker is turned in the throwing phase.
- The type of grip is optional.

1. A applies a frontal headlock.
2. D counters with a right-handed jab at A's neck.
3. D frees himself from the grip with his left arm pulls his head free grabs between A's legs with his right arm and lays the right hand on A's bottom/lower back, the

left hand is placed diagonally over the right neck side on to A's back.D lifts A up by stretching up from his knees turns him in to the horizontal position...

5. ...and lets him drop...

6. ...and goes down on top of him in the straddle position...

7. ...sliding the right knee up over A's left upper arm...

8. ...placing his left foot next to A's left ear (the heel is pointing at the neck) and applies a stretched arm lock over the groin to immobilize the opponent.

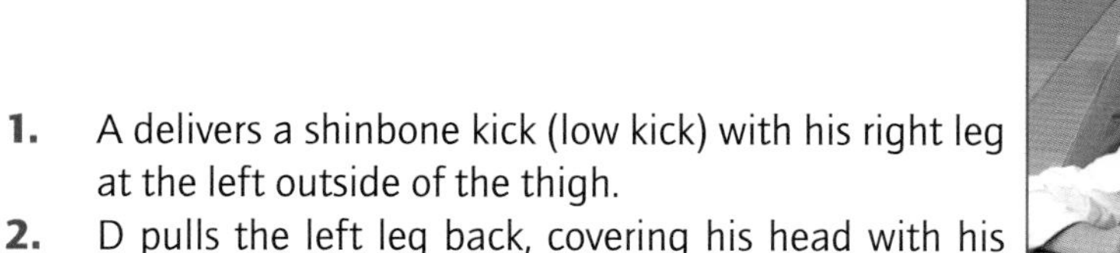

1. A delivers a shinbone kick (low kick) with his right leg at the left outside of the thigh.
2. D pulls the left leg back, covering his head with his left hand and sweeps the right leg with his right leg further outwards.
3. D is now standing behind A.
   D grabs between A's legs with his right arm and places the hand on A's stomach and grabbing with his left arm over A's back, placing the hand on A's chest.
4. D lifts A, stretching up from his knees turns A into a horizontal position...
5. ...and lets him drop on to his stomach.
6. D gets onto A's back, pushes both of his legs under A's legs and grabs under A's neck with his right arm. He then lays the right hand on A's left shoulder,
7. the back of the left hand on the back of his head/neck and by tensing the arm as well as applying pressure forwards a stranglehold is effected.

1. A delivers a left-fisted punch at D's head. D counters by sweeping this down to the inside with his right hand.

2. A delivers a right-fisted punch (jab) at D's head.
D counters by sweeping this down to the inside with his left hand.

3. ...grasps between A's legs with the right hand and pulls A's right sleeve with his left hand...

4-5. ...and takes him up onto his shoulders.

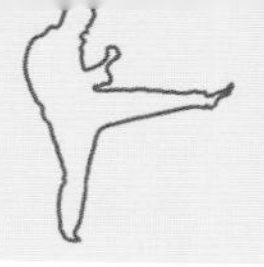

6. D straightens himself up (shoulder wheel lift) and closes his left leg to his right leg.

7. By pulling on the right arm and applying pressure with the right hand, A is thrown down to the left.

8-9. D turns A over on to his stomach...

10-11. ...and carries out a cross lock (bent arm lock) with the leg to immobilize A.

7.6.4 Sweeping hip throw (Harai-goshi) or thigh throw (Uchi-mata)

- Put the opponent off balance by pulling forwards and/or carrying out an Atemi technique.
- The type of grip to be used is optional.
- Turn in and duck under the opponent's center of gravity.

Sweeping hip throw (Harai-goshi)

Simultaneously stretching the standing leg and sweeping the opponent's leg using the thigh from the outside.

1. A applies a stranglehold with both hands from a sideways position on the right.
2. D counters with an elbow strike sideways and to the right into A's stomach grasps hold inside of A's right sleeve with his left hand...

3. ...grabs round A's hips with his right arm pulls A on to his right hip...

4. ...and sweeps up A onto the hip.
He then pulls A's right arm with his left hand.
When executing the throw, D pulls his left wrist as if he was looking at his watch.
The right leg is placed against A's right thigh. The upper body is bent and the right leg is swung up backwards.

5. D throws A with the sweeping hip throw down to the ground.
The left hand pulls the wrist upwards, while the right hand is applying hard pressure on the right elbow joint so that A arches his back in pain.

6. In this position, D brings the stretched-out arm in the direction of the ground and with a stretched arm lock immobilizes A.

1. Standing with his left leg leading, A delivers a left-fisted punch (jab) at D's head.
D executes a sweeping block with the hand.

2. A then follows this up with a further right-fisted punch at D's head.
D counters with a sweeping block with the left arm.

3. The left hand grabs hold of A's right sleeve.

4. D turns round counterclockwise grabs A round the thigh with his right arm...

5-6. ...pulling A's body on to his hip and executes a hip throw: Pulling on the right arm with his left hand. When executing the throw D looks at his left wrist as if to look at his watch. The right leg is placed against A's right thigh. The upper body is bent and the right leg is swung up backwards.

7. D kneels down with his left knee on A's head and the right knee down to the side. He maintains control by applying a bent hand lock.

1. A executes a strike with a stick coming in downwards and inwards at D's head.
2. D sweeps the weapon bearing hand downwards and outwards with his left hand delivering at the same time a right-handed finger jab (disrupting action) at the eyes...
3. ...and wraps the left hand round the arm with the weapon...
4. ...disarming him with the 'snake' movement.
5. D grabs hold of A's right sleeve with his left hand holding on to A's thigh with his right hand...
6. ...pulls A on his own hip.

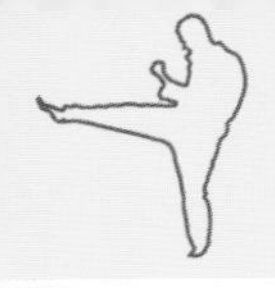

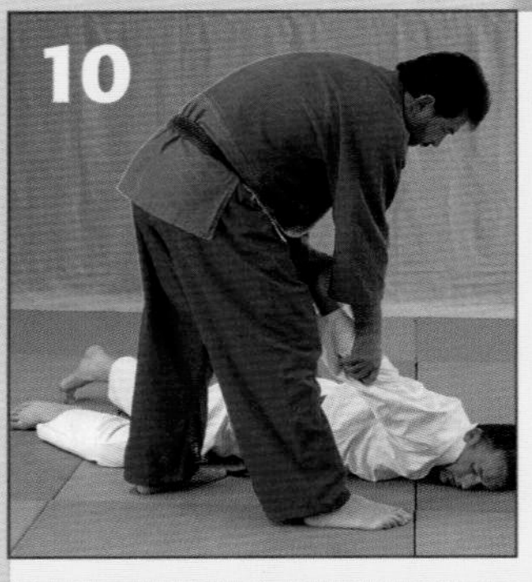

7. ...and executes a hip throw: Pulling on the right arm with his left hand. When executing the throw D looks at his left wrist as if to look at his watch. The right leg is placed against A's right thigh. The upper body is bent and the right leg is swung up backwards.

8-10. D turns A over on to his stomach...

11. ...bends A's right arm inwards slightly...

12. ...grabs hold of A's right hand with his right hand and places the left hand in the area of the triceps.

13. D now pulls the right arm upwards, so that the bent hand lock takes effect...

14. ...pinning the opponent's right arm between his own chest and the right hand and presses A's head with his left hand in the direction of A's left shoulder.

Thigh throw (Uchi-mata)

Simultaneously stretching the standing leg, which has been brought well under the center of balance, and bending the own upper body forwards, swinging the free leg between the opponent's legs backwards and upwards; the throw can be executed either as a leg or a hip throw.

1-3. A delivers a shinbone kick at D's left thigh with his right foot.
D counters with a defensive action using his left lower leg sweeping outwards...

4. ...followed by an uppercut at A's chin with his right fist.

5. At the same time, he grabs hold of the right sleeve with his left hand and with his right hand he grabs the collar.

6. D pulls hard with both arms allowing him to place his left foot in front and near to A's left foot.

8

9

10

11

12

13

14

7. A is pulled forward on to the hip. The left leg is bent.
The right leg is placed by A's right thigh.
Both legs are stretched upwards and D's upper body is bent well forwards (A's genital area is directly on D's right thigh).
D turns left and looks at his left wrist (as if looking at his watch) and A is thrown forward.

8-10. D turns A over on to his stomach...

11. ...and grabs hold of A's finger with his right hand to apply a finger lock.

12-14. A's right elbow is pinned down by D's upper arm and the left hand pushes A's head in the direction of his left shoulder.

1. A delivers an in-swinging punch with his right fist.
2. D counters executing a left forearm block outwards and at the same time delivering an uppercut at A's chin.
3. D grabs hold of A's sleeve with his left hand and with his right hand he grabs A's collar.
   D pulls hard with both arms allowing him to place his left foot in front and near to A's left foot.
4. A is pulled forward on to the hip.
   The left leg is bent and the right leg is bent and placed between A's legs.
   By stretching both legs upwards A is lifted up...

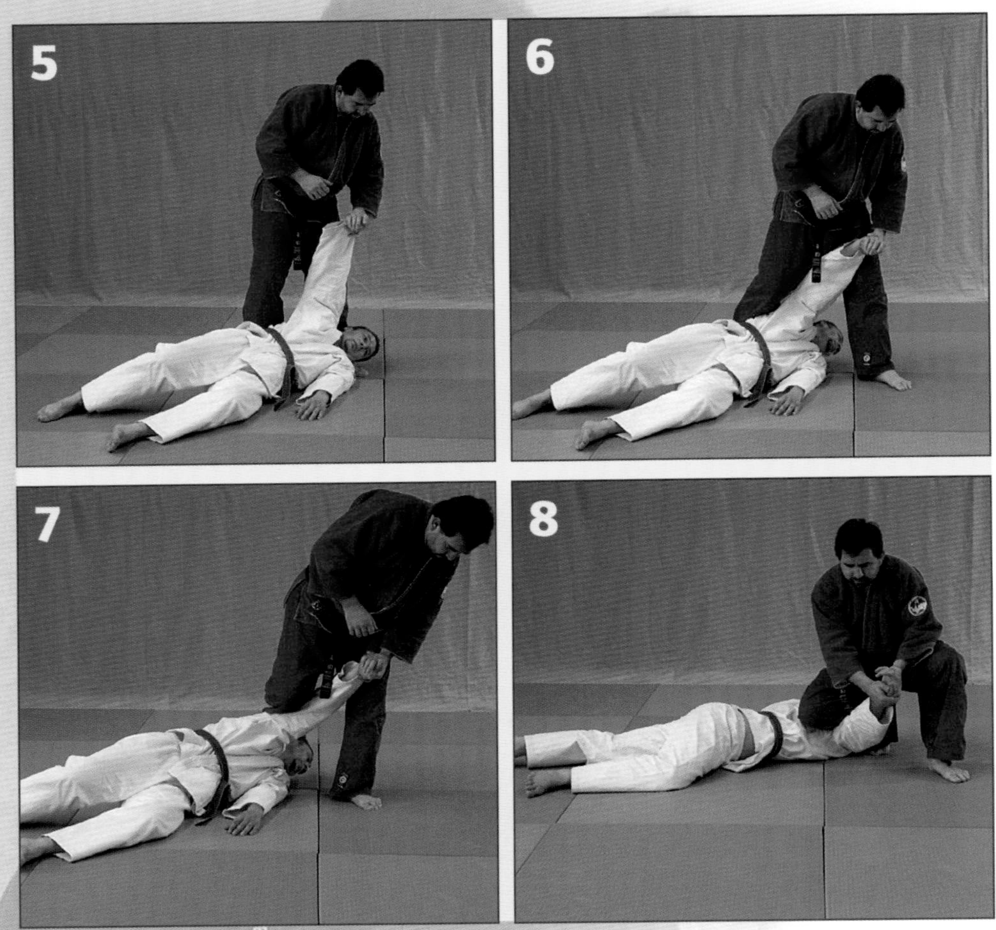

5. ...and by doing a turning movement (D looks at his left wrist (as if looking at his watch)) A is thrown forward.
6. D steps over A's head with his left foot first...
7. ...places the right foot on A's right upper arm...
8. ...turns A on to his stomach and immobilizes him with a stretched arm lock.

8 Defense against Stick Attacks

8.1 Controlling the stick attacking arm

- Defense against stick attacks Numbers 1-8 by taking hold of the attacking arm combined with appropriate dodging maneuvers.

- Control of the arm holding the weapon using the free hand or both hands.

- Additional follow-on techniques are optional.

When controlling the arm holding the weapon, it can be said that control actually has been achieved when the attacker is not able to move his wrist anymore. When only the elbow is being controlled, the attacker can possibly make a strike using his wrist (also known as an *Abanico*, i.e., *fan strike*).

When defending against weapons the following principles should be noted:
Forearm blocks are always carried out with the flat of the hand showing to the ground. In the defense against sticks this does not play any particular role. However, when defending against knife attacks, even minor injuries can be caused when the knife is pulled back. Where the defender finds himself on the inside in an attack, he tries to get to the outside of the attacking arm. If he is already on the outside of the arm, he stays in that position. As a general rule, the opposite (i.e., the one facing the opponent) arm is used for the defense being the nearest to the arm holding the weapon. This is because the natural reflexes can be put to best use that way. As soon as the techniques–as described in the following sections–have been perfected, practicing defense against the diagonally opposite weapon bearing arm should be started. This type of defense represents a greater challenge on the defender's co-ordination skills, because when the centerline of the body is crossed by the arm, the opposite side of the brain has to take over control.

Attack No. 1 — Diagonal strike from the right downwards and inwards at D's head

1. D executes a left forearm block outwards to the left. The hand remains open but the arm is tensed.
2. D places the back of the right hand on A's right arm...
3. ...and sweeps the arm holding the weapon counterclockwise downwards and outwards to the right.
4. D's left hand is holding underneath A's elbow
5. and the right hand is directly on top of A's elbow.
   The fingers of the right hand are aiming a finger jab at A's right eye.
   Pressure on the weapon bearing hand is directed towards A's left shoulder so that a strike using the left hand is no longer possible.
6. D grabs hold of A's right wrist with his right hand places the left hand on the right elbow and takes control of the arm holding the weapon.

Attack No. 2 — Diagonal strike from the left downwards and inwards at D's head

1. D executes a right forearm block. The hand is open but the forearm is tensed. The flat of the hand is showing towards the ground.
2. D's left hand is holding underneath A's elbow
3. and the right hand is directly on top of A's elbow. The fingers of the right hand are aiming a finger jab at A's right eye. Pressure on the weapon bearing hand is directed towards A's left shoulder so that a strike using the left hand is no longer possible.
4. D grabs hold of A's right wrist with his right hand...
5. ...places the left hand on the right elbow and takes control of the arm holding the weapon.

Attack No. 3—Horizontal strike with the right hand from the right inwards at D's hip

1. D executes a left forearm block downwards and outwards. The hand is open but the forearm is tensed. The flat of the hand is showing towards the ground.
2. D places the back of the right hand on A's right arm and sweeps the weapon bearing arm counterclockwise downwards and outwards to the right.
3. D's left hand is holding underneath A's elbow
4. and the right hand is directly on top of A's elbow.
5. The fingers of the right hand are aiming a finger jab at A's right eye.
   Pressure on the weapon bearing hand is directed towards A's left shoulder so that a strike using the left hand is no longer possible.
6. D grabs hold of A's right wrist with his right hand places the left hand on the right elbow and takes control of the arm holding the weapon.

Attack No. 4 — Horizontal strike with the right hand from the left inwards at D's hip

1. D executes a right forearm block downwards and outwards. The hand is open but the forearm is tensed. The flat of the hand is showing towards the ground.
2. D's left hand is holding underneath A's elbow
3. and the right hand is directly on top of A's elbow. The fingers of the right hand are aiming a finger jab at A's right eye. Pressure on the weapon bearing hand is directed towards A's left shoulder so that a strike using the left hand is no longer possible.
4. D grabs hold of A's right wrist with his right hand...

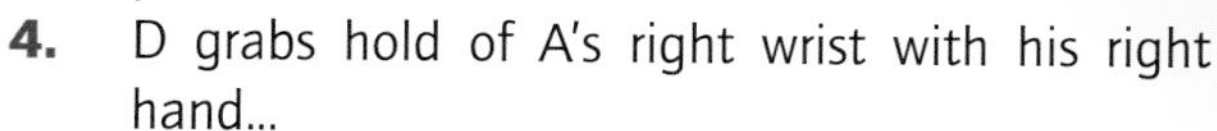

5. ...places the left hand on the right elbow and takes control of the arm holding the weapon.

Attack No. 5—Stick strike at D's stomach

1. D executes a right forearm block downwards and outwards. The hand is open but the forearm is tensed. The flat of the hand is showing towards the ground.
2. D's left hand is holding underneath A's elbow
3. and the right hand is directly on top of A's elbow. The fingers of the right hand are aiming a finger jab at A's right eye.
   Pressure on the weapon bearing hand is directed towards A's left shoulder so that a strike using the left hand is no longer possible.
4. D grabs hold of A's right wrist with his right hand...
5. ...places the left hand on the right elbow and takes control of the arm holding the weapon.

Attack No. 6 – Horizontal strike downwards at D's head

1. D blocks the attacking arm with his left forearm,
2. sweeps the attacking arm with his right arm away clockwise...
3. ...downwards and outwards to the right.
4. D's left hand is holding underneath A's elbow
5. and the right hand is directly on top of A's elbow. The fingers of the right hand are aiming a finger jab at A's right eye.
   Pressure on the weapon bearing hand is directed towards A's left shoulder so that a strike using the left hand is no longer possible.
6. D grabs hold of A's right wrist with his right hand...
7. ...places the left hand on the right elbow and takes control of the arm holding the weapon.

Attack No. 7—Diagonal strike from the right to the left downwards at D's legs

1. D pulls the forward leg backwards, blocks with his left forearm...

2-3. ...and sweeps the attacking arm with his right arm away clockwise, downwards and outwards to the right.

4. D's left hand is holding underneath A's elbow

5. and the right hand is directly on top of A's elbow. The fingers of the right hand are aiming a finger jab at A's right eye.

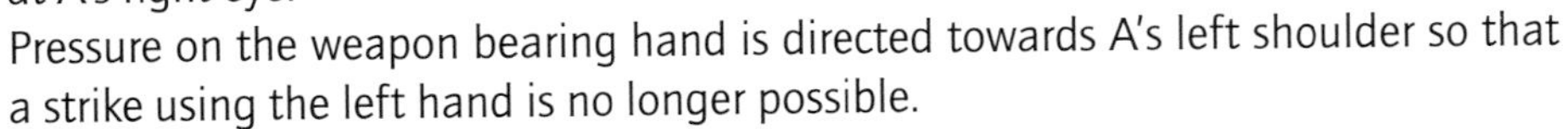
Pressure on the weapon bearing hand is directed towards A's left shoulder so that a strike using the left hand is no longer possible.

6. D grabs hold of A's right wrist with his right hand...

7. ...places the left hand on the right elbow and takes control of the arm holding the weapon.

Attack No. 8 — Diagonal strike downwards from the left to the right at D's legs

1. D pulls the forward right leg backwards and blocks the attacking arm with his right arm away, downwards and outwards.
2. D's left hand is holding underneath A's elbow
3. and the right hand is directly on top of A's elbow.
   The fingers of the right hand are aiming a finger jab at A's right eye.
   Pressure on the weapon bearing hand is directed towards A's left shoulder so that a strike using the left hand is no longer possible.
4. D grabs hold of A's right wrist with his right hand...
5. ...places the left hand on the right elbow and takes control of the arm holding the weapon.

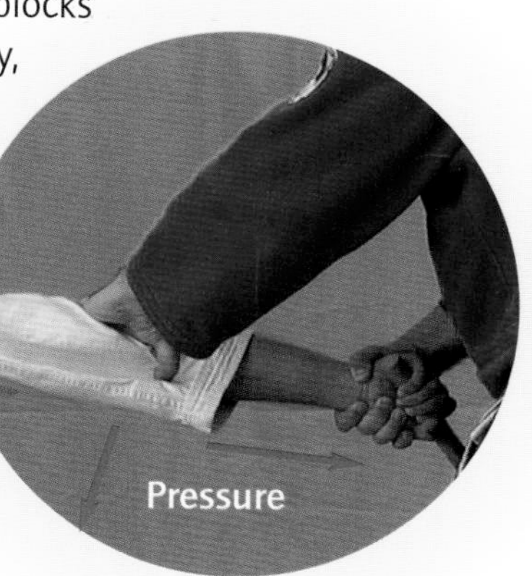

8.2 Counter-attacks & disturbing techniques against stick attacks

- Defense against stick attacks Numbers 1-8 by taking hold of the attacking arm combined with appropriate dodging maneuvers.
- At the same time as the holding action is done, an Atemi technique is executed to disrupt the attacker or to prepare for a follow-on technique (e.g., a finger jab to the hollow of the larynx).
- Control of the arm holding the weapon using the free hand or both hands.
- Additional follow-on techniques are optional.

Attack Series No. 1 (from the outside to the head)

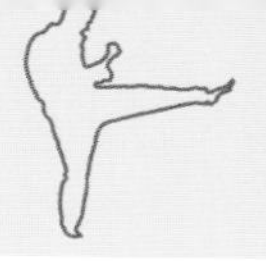

1. A strikes from the outside to the head.
2. D executes a left forearm block outwards and at the same time delivers a finger jab (disrupting action) with his right hand at the eyes.
3. With his right hand, D brings A's right arm further downwards and inwards...
4. ...and grabs A's right hand (ball of the thumb) with his left hand (controlling the weapon bearing arm)...

5-6. ...disarms him with the forearm...

7-8. ...and applies a bent hand lock to bring him down to the ground.

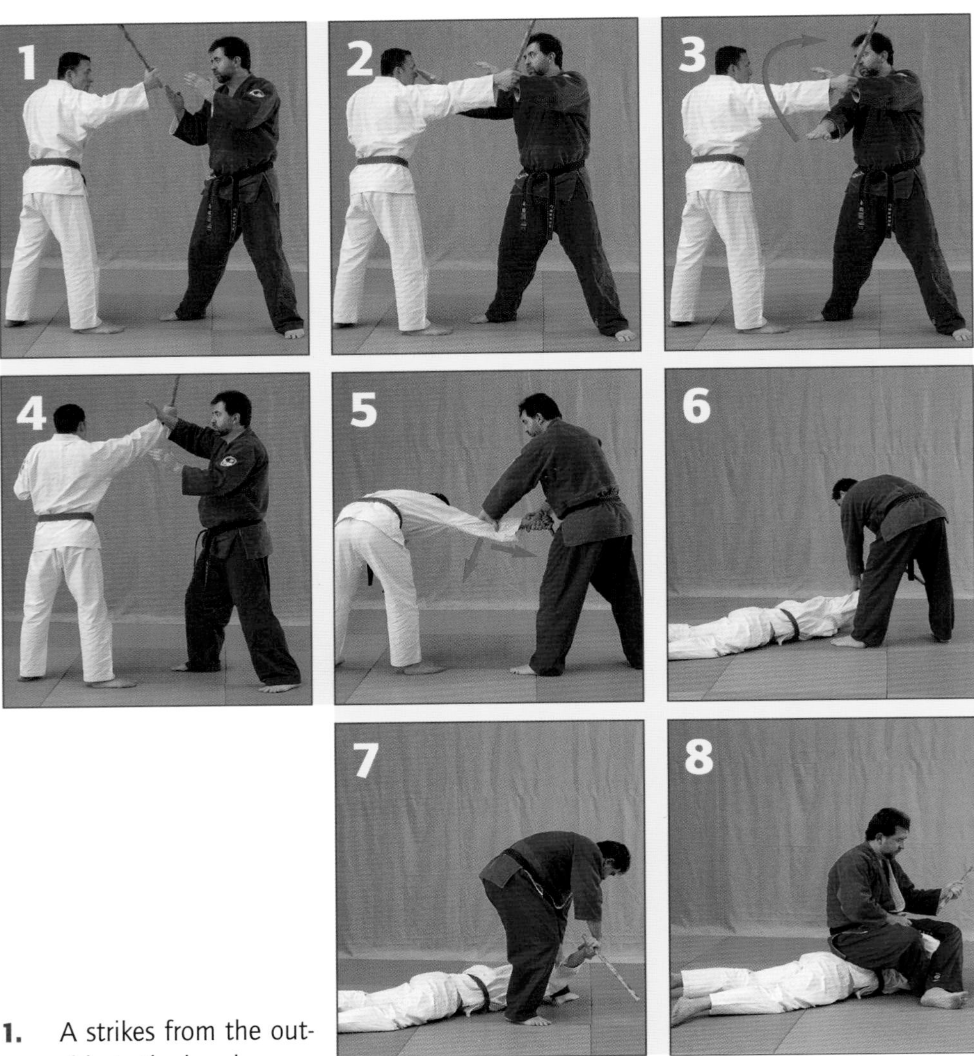

1. A strikes from the outside to the head.
2. D executes a left forearm block out-wards and at the same time delivers a finger jab (disrupting action) with his right hand at the eyes.

3-4. With his right hand, D brings A's right arm further upwards and inwards...

5. ...and applies a stretched arm lock (D's right hand is controlling the weapon bearing hand)...
6. ...and brings A in this way down to the ground.
7. D steps over A's outstretched arm with the left leg...
8. ...sits down on A's back disarms him using his hand and immobilizes him using a bent arm lock.

1. A strikes from the outside to the head.
2. D sweeps the weapon bearing hand diagonally downwards and outwards to the right with his right hand, while at the same time delivering a left-handed finger jab (disrupting action) into the eyes.
3. The left hand takes control of the elbow...
4. ...and at the same time a second finger jab is delivered to the eyes with the right hand.
5. The right hand grabs hold of the right wrist (controlling the weapon bearing arm)...
6. ...and the left arm is pushed underneath A's right arm in order to carry out a stretched arm lock over the upper arm.

Attack Series No. 2 (from the inside to the head)

2. D executes an arm-breaking blow (disrupting action) with his left hand, controlling the right wrist at the same time with his right hand.
3. With his right hand, D brings A's right hand downwards and inwards...
4. ...and brings this further behind A...

6. ...and pulls it back again—jamming the stick between A's legs and disarms A using this method of the body.
7. D reaches over A's right arm with the left arm...
8. ...'coils' A's right arm round his left arm...
9. ...and ends the combination with a coiled arm lock.

1. A strikes from the inside to the head.

2. D counters with a lefthanded swap outwards while at the same time delivering a finger jab at the eyes with his right hand.

3. ...and a twisting stretched arm lock is applied (controlling the weapon bearing arm).

4-5. D disarms A with his right hand...

6. ...and bends A's right arm onto his back in a bent arm lock...

7. ...and then places the lower end of the stick on the left side of A's neck.

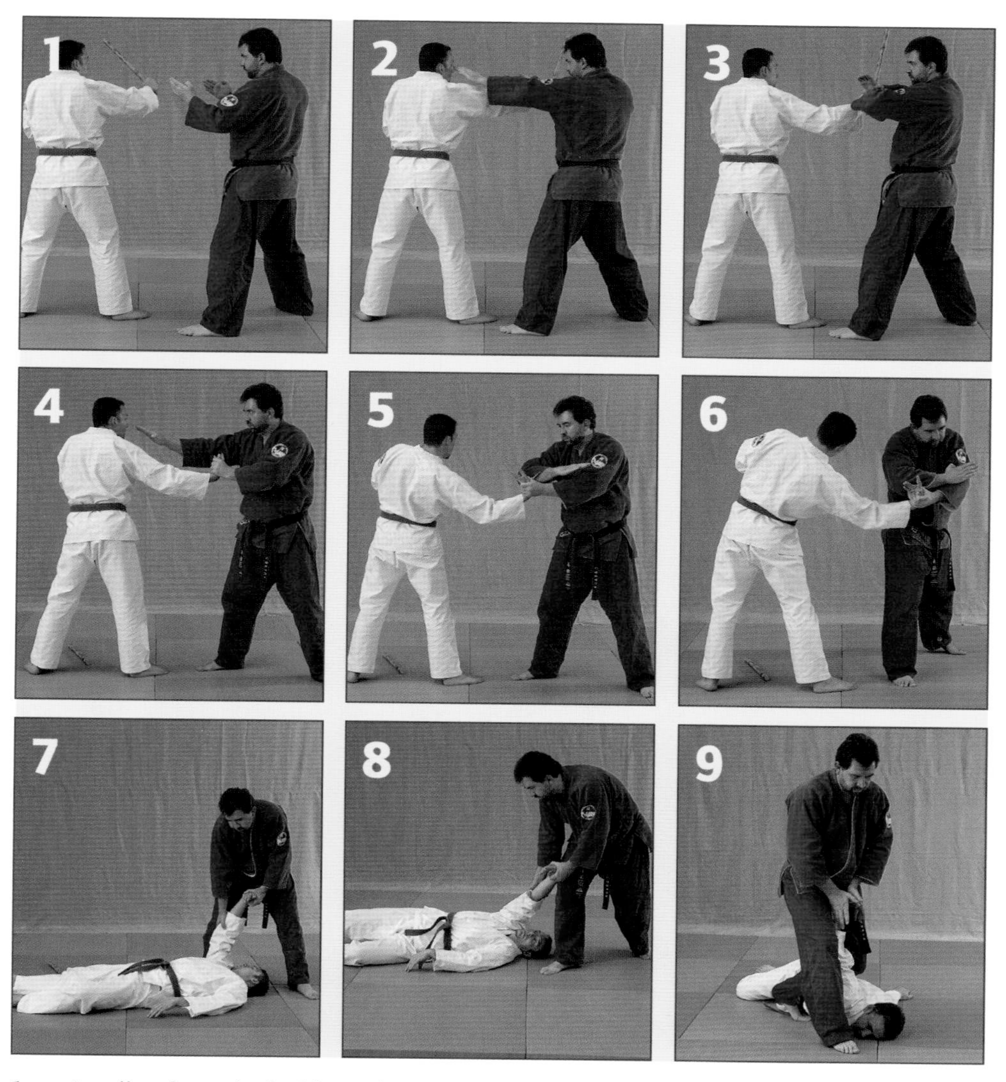

1. A strikes from the inside to the head.

2. D counters with a right forearm block outwards while at the same time delivering a finger jab (disrupting action) with his left hand at the eyes.

3. The left hand grabs hold of the ball of the right thumb. The right forearm is placed on the stick...

4. ...and the disarming action takes place over the forearm. As this is done the right hand is brought up further towards A's eyes and a finger jab is delivered at the eyes.

5-6. After this D places his forearm on the back of A's hand...

7. ...and brings him in the direction of the ground using a bent hand lock over the forearm in combination with a step turn.
8. D places the right hand on A's right elbow...
9. ...and turns him over on to his stomach placing his left knee between A's shoulder blades:
- D pins the stretched-out right arm between his legs.
- D pushes his hips forward...
- ...and executes a twisting bent hand lock with the hands.

Attack Series No. 3 (from the outside au hip height)

1. D counters with a sweeping block inwards with the left arm,
2. while at the same time taking a step backwards with the left foot

3. and delivering a right-handed finger jab (disrupting action) at A's eyes.
4. The right hand takes hold of A's right wrist
5. and the left hand holds the right elbow.
6. Using a stretched arm lock, D executes a controlling action.

1. A strikes from the outside at hip height.

2. D counters with a left forearm block downwards and outwards delivering a right-handed finger jab (disrupting action) at the same time.

3-5. D then comes up with the left arm from below upwards round the weapon bearing arm to 'slip' into a twisting stretch lock (controlling the weapon arm).

1. A strikes from the outside at hip height.
2. D carries out a diagonal sweeping block inwards with the right hand while at the same time delivering a finger jab (disrupting action) at the eyes.
3. The left hand takes over holding the right wrist (controlling the weapon bearing arm)...
4. ...and the right hand grabs hold of A's right hand.
   Using a bent hand lock the hand holding the weapon is brought under control.

Attack Series No. 4 (from the inside at hip height)

1. A strikes from the inside at hip height.
2. D carries out a diagonal sweeping block outwards with the left hand while at the same time delivering a finger jab (disrupting action) at the eyes with the right hand.
3. The right hand grabs hold of A's right hand...
4. ...and uses a twisting bent hand lock.

1. A strikes from the inside at hip height.
2. D counters by carrying out a right forearm block downwards and outwards with the right hand while at the same time delivering a finger jab (disrupting action) at the eyes with the left hand...
3. ...bringing the weapon bearing arm downwards and inwards with the left arm...

4-5. ...and using a twisting stretched lock (stretched arm lock) the arm holding the weapon is brought under control.

1. A strikes from the inside at hip height.
2. D counters by carrying out a right forearm block downwards and outwards with the right hand while at the same time delivering a finger jab (disrupting action) at the eyes with the left hand.
3. Using the left hand he takes hold of A's right wrist (controlling the weapon bearing arm).
4. Using the right hand he grabs the right hand and applies a bent hand lock.

Attack Series No. 5 (strike with the stick at the stomach)

1. A strikes with the stick at the stomach.
2. D carries out an edge of the hand block (reverse Salute block), i.e., a chop with the right hand downwards while at the same time delivering a left-handed finger jab (disrupting action) at the eyes.
3. The left hand grabs hold of A's right wrist...
4. ...turns the hand counterclockwise outwards grabs hold of the right hand with his right hand and applies a bent hand lock.

1. A strikes with the stick at the stomach.

2. D carries out an edge of the hand block (reverse Salute block), i.e., a chop with the right hand downwards while at the same time delivering a left-handed finger jab (disrupting action) at the eyes.
As he does this he presses the left forearm against A's right forearm.

3. D's right hand grabs hold of the ball of A's right thumb.

4-5. The left hand is placed on the elbow...

6. ...and A is brought down to the ground with a stretched arm lock (controlling the weapon bearing hand) and is immobilized.

1. A strikes with the stick at the stomach.
2. D executes a left forearm block outwards and at the same time delivers a finger jab (disrupting action) with his right hand at the eyes.
3. With his right hand, D grabs hold of A's right wrist (controlling the weapon bearing hand)...
4. ...and applies a bent hand lock.

Attack Series No. 6 (downwards at the head)

1. A strikes downwards at the head.

2-3. D carries out a sweeping block outwards with his right hand, while at the same time delivering a left-handed finger jab at the eyes.

4. D places the left hand underneath the elbow
5. and executes a further finger jab with his right hand at A's eyes.
6. The right hand grabs hold of the ball of A's right thumb (controlling the weapon bearing arm)...
7. ...places the left hand on the right elbow and applies a stretched arm lock.
8. Using the stretched arm lock he forces A down to the ground and immobilizes him.

1. A strikes downwards at the head.

2-3. D carries out a sweeping block outwards with his right hand, while at the same time delivering a left-handed finger jab at the eyes.

4. D places the left hand underneath the elbow.
The right hand grabs hold of the ball of A's right thumb (controlling the weapon bearing arm).

5. D brings the left arm over A's right arm and takes hold of his own right wrist.

6. Using a bent arm lock A is brought under control.

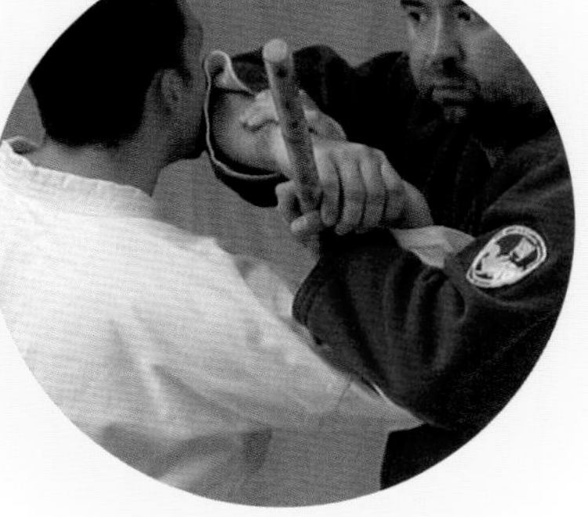

1. A strikes downwards at the head.
2. D carries out a sweeping block outwards with his left hand, while at the same time delivering a right-handed finger jab at the eyes (disrupting action).
3. D brings A's weapon bearing arm in a circle downwards, inwards and then upwards with his left hand.
4. A stretched arm lock over the shoulder (controlling the weapon bearing arm) ends the combination.

Attack Series No. 7 (from outwards at the legs)

1. A strikes outwards at the legs.
2. D brings his left front leg rearwards and lets the stick go past him. At the same time D sweeps the arm outwards with his right arm and delivers a left-handed finger jab (disrupting action) at A's head.
3. The left hand grabs hold of A's right hand (ball of the thumb) (controlling the weapon bearing hand).
4. The right hand grabs hold of A's right hand and applies a bent hand lock.

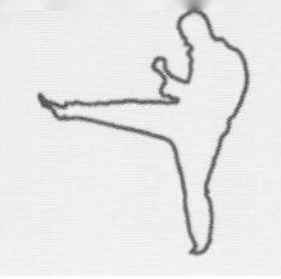

1. A strikes outwards at the legs.
2. D brings his left front leg rearwards and lets the stick go whizzing past him and at the same time sweeps the weapon bearing arm inwards with his left arm.
3. D places the left hand underneath A's right elbow and delivers a right-handed finger jab (disrupting action) at A's eyes.
4. With his right hand D grabs hold of the weapon bearing hand (controlling it),

5-6. grasps round with the left hand and applies pressure on the elbow (stretched arm lock) (control of the arm holding the weapon).

1. A strikes outwards at the legs.
2. D brings his left front leg rearwards and at the same time executes a left forearm block downwards and outwards to the left.
3. D brings the weapon bearing arm outwards to the right with his right hand...
4. ...places the left hand underneath A's left elbow
5. and at the same time delivers a right-handed finger jab (disrupting action) at A's eyes.
6. With his right hand D grabs hold of the weapon bearing hand (controlling it)...
7. ...and reaches over A's right arm with his left arm and takes hold of his own right wrist.
8. D immobilizes A with a bent arm lock.

Attack Series No. 8 (from inside at the legs)

1. A strikes from the inside at the legs.
   D brings his left front leg rearwards...
2. ...and sweeps the weapon bearing hand with his left hand to the left and outwards, while at the same time delivering a right-handed finger jab (disrupting action) at A's head.
3. With his right hand D grabs hold of A's right hand (controlling the weapon bearing hand)
4. and applies a twisting bent hand lock.

1. A strikes from the inside at the legs.
2. D brings his left front leg rearwards...
3. ...and sweeps the weapon bearing hand with his left hand outwards, while at the same time delivering a right-handed finger jab (disrupting action) at A's eyes.
4. D brings the left hand underneath A's right hand lays the left hand on A's right elbow lays the right hand on top of this...
5. ...and applies a twisting stretch lock (controlling the weapon bearing hand).

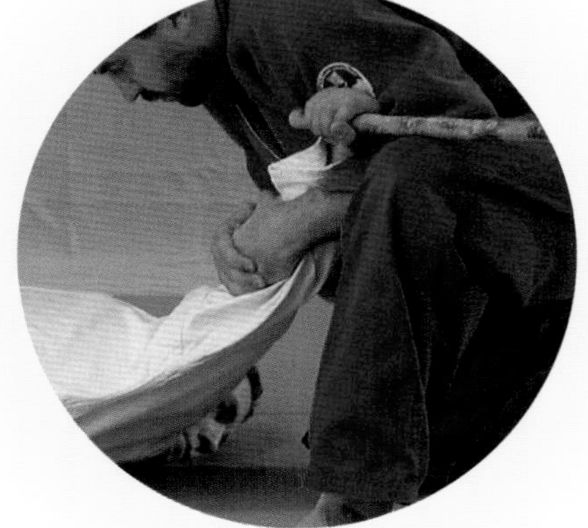

1. A strikes from the inside at the legs.
2. D carries out a forearm block downwards and outwards to the right, while at the same time delivering a finger jab to the left at the eyes and taking a lunging step 45° forwards left.
3. The left hand grabs hold of A's right hand.
4. The right hand also grabs hold of A's right hand and applies a bent hand lock as a controlling action.

9 Defense against Knife Attacks

9.1 Controlling the knife attacking arm

- Defense against knife attacks Numbers 1-5 by taking hold of the attacking arm combined with appropriate dodging maneuvers.
- Here, only the way of holding the knife in stabbing and cutting attacks (i.e., blade is on the thumb side of the hand) is covered. Defense against attacks where the handle is grasped from above (i.e., blade is on the little finger side of the hand) should, however, also be practiced.
- Control of the arm holding the weapon using the free hand or both hands.
- Additional follow-on techniques are optional.

In this section, the focus is on controlling the weapon bearing arm. Disarming and disrupting techniques are covered in later volumes.

Here, a system is taught that makes it possible for the pupil to be able to learn these techniques fairly quickly. All the types of defense are based on the following common principles:

- Blocking is done using the nearest hand to the weapon in order to make best use of the natural reflexes.
- If, after carrying out the block, the defender is standing on the inside, he moves to the outside.
- If, after carrying out the block, the defender is standing on the outside, he stays outside.
- The palm of the hand is always showing towards the ground, in order to avoid serious knife injuries when the knife is pulled back.

Attack No. 1 (from the outside at the neck)

1. A strikes at the neck from the outside.

1

2. Using the three-step contact, D carries out a block left.

3. Sweeping action outwards to the right.

4. Controlling with the left–A's weapon bearing hand outwards to the right.

5. D's left hand is placed underneath A's elbow and the right hand is placed on top of the elbow.
With a right-handed finger jab, D threatens A's right eye.
Pressure on the weapon bearing arm is applied towards A's left shoulder so that a strike using the left hand is no longer possible.

Attack No. 2 (from the inside at the neck)

1. A strikes at the neck from the inside.
2. D blocks the weapon bearing arm with his right hand.
3. D's left hand is placed underneath A's elbow and the right hand is placed directly on top of the elbow.
   With a right-handed finger jab, D threatens A's right eye.
   Pressure on the weapon bearing arm is applied towards A's left shoulder so that a strike using the left hand is no longer possible.

Attack No. 3 (from the outside at hip height)

1. A strikes at hip height from the outside.
2. Using the three-step contact, D carries out a block left, downwards and outwards.
3. Sweeping action outwards to the right.
4. Controlling with the left–A's weapon bearing hand outwards to the right.
5. D's left hand is placed underneath A's elbow and the right hand is placed on top of the elbow.
   With a right-handed finger jab, D threatens A's right eye.
   Pressure on the weapon bearing arm is applied towards A's left shoulder so that a strike using the left hand is no longer possible.

Attack No. 4 (from the inside at hip height)

1. A strikes at hip height from the inside.
2. D blocks the weapon bearing arm with his right hand.
3. D's left hand is placed underneath A's elbow...
   ...and the right hand is placed directly on top of A's elbow. With a right-handed finger jab, D threatens A's right eye.
   Pressure on the weapon bearing arm is applied towards A's left shoulder so that a strike using the left hand is no longer possible.

Attack No. 5 (strike at the stomach)

1. A strikes at the stomach.
2. D blocks the weapon bearing arm with his right hand.
3. D's left hand is placed underneath A's elbow and the right hand is placed directly on top of A's elbow. With a right-handed finger jab, D threatens A's right eye. Pressure on the weapon bearing arm is applied towards A's left shoulder so that a strike using the left hand is no longer possible.

When these techniques have been mastered, the following can be adapted for used in combination with Attack No's 1 and 3:

1. D carries out a sweeping block with his right hand counterclockwise downwards and outwards...
2. ...and then places the left hand underneath A's elbow and the right hand directly on top of A's elbow.
3. With a right-handed finger jab, D threatens A's right eye.
4. Pressure on the weapon bearing arm is applied towards A's left shoulder so that a strike using the left hand is no longer possible.

9.2 Training Methods

Phase 1

1. A is standing behind D with a knife in his hand.
2. A calls out which attack angle he will use and gives D time to work out which combination he will reply with (4-5 seconds).
3. When A says, "NOW", D turns round.
4. A now executes the attack he has announced.

Phase 2

D keeps his eyes closed all the time and A reduces the speed of the beginning of the attack.

10 Defense against Attacks with Various Objects

- The pupil chooses a type of attack, once with contact (e.g., stranglehold with a chain) and once without contact (e.g., strike inwards with a whip cane).
- The type of defense used is optional.

10.1 With contact

1

1. From one side, A wraps a chain round D pinning his arms.
2. D reaches round A's hips with his right arm...
3. ...pulls A in close to him...
4. ...and throws him with a hip throw forwards.
5-6. A kick down with the foot ends the combination.

1. A applies a stranglehold with the chain from the front.
2. D grabs hold of A's neck with both hands and delivers a head butt...
3. ...followed by a knee kick into the genital area.
4-5. D gets out of the noose by slipping his head to the left under the chain.
6. D grabs hold of the wrist with his right hand and the elbow with his left hand...
7. ...and forces A down to the ground using a stretched arm lock.
8. D grabs hold of the left wrist with his right hand and the elbow joint with his left hand...
9. ...and moves A about with a bent hand lock.

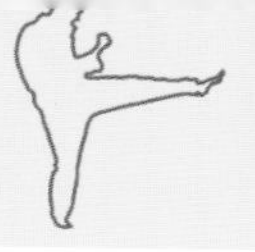

1. A applies a stranglehold with the chain from behind.
2. D falls, dropping backwards.
3. D grabs hold of A's neck/head with both hands
4. and pulls A with him down to the ground.
D delivers a knee kick at A's head...
5-6. ...turns him onto his back with a neck lock...
7-8. disarms A, and ends the combination with a punch at A's head.

10.2 Without contact

1. A executes a strike with the chain inwards from the right at D's head.

2-4. D carries out a three-step contact (left block–bringing the arm to the right outwards with the right hand–controlling the right arm by applying pressure on the elbow with his left hand) thus bringing the weapon bearing arm onto the right side and ducking his head.

5. D pulls A down to the ground with a stretched arm lock...
6. ...and immobilizes him, disarming him.

1. A executes a strike with the chain outwards.
2. D does a quick block with his right arm
3. and brings the weapon bearing arm further outwards to the left with his left arm (D is ducking as he does this)...
4. ...slips with his left hand over A's upper arm and places his hand on the triceps. After this, D delivers an elbow strike at A's chin...
5. ...places his right leg behind A's right leg and trips him over.
6. D pulls the wrist with his left hand...
7. ...presses the right hand against the elbow (stretched arm lock) so that A arches his back in pain.
8. D immobilizes A on the ground with a stretched arm lock and disarms him.

1. A executes a chain strike down onto D's head.
2. D stretches his right arm out and positions it a few centimeters behind A's weapon bearing hand.
3. The chain wraps itself round D's wrist and in the best case it continues wrapping round the wrist so that the end strikes A's hand.
4. Otherwise, D rips the chain out of A's grip...
5. ...while at the same time D delivers a finger jab at the eyes...
6. ...placing the right foot to the rear and ending the combination with a left-legged shinbone kick (low-kick) at A's forward thigh.

11 Follow-on Techniques

11.1 Follow-on techniques after a locking technique

- As chosen freely by the pupil, the execution of a follow-on technique for each of two locking techniques with opponent reaction.
- For the follow-on, the energy used by the opponent in his reaction should be used in the defense further.

In the sections of Follow-on and Counter measure techniques for locking actions, I would like to introduce a form of training of a sequence of locks, which are required normally when testing for the higher belt grades. This form of training allows the pupil to memorize and apply them relatively quickly.

Counter measures and follow-on techniques in the form of a sequence of locking actions

1. A delivers a punch with the ball of the right hand at D's right shoulder. D turns slightly backwards,
2. reaches over A's arm with his left arm, takes hold of the hand
3. and applies a bent hand lock.
4. A pushes D's right hand to the left with his left hand
5. and applies a bent hand lock (counter measure technique).
6. D strikes A's right hand downwards away with the back of the left hand/the forearm
7. and directly applies a twisting stretch lock. This is a follow-on from the failed bent hand lock and at the same time a counter measure against the bent hand lock. The following sequence can be seen as the same and therefore will not be covered further. All the combinations can, of course, also be practiced individually.

8. A angles the right arm by first of all pulling it back and then turning it upwards so that his own little finger is pointing at the ceiling.

9. D avoids the bent arm lock by delivering a punch with the ball of the right hand at A's right shoulder.

10. A dodges back with the right shoulder and carries out a 'Salute' block with the right hand,

11. grabbing hold of D's right hand and directly executing a twisting hand lock.

12. D knocks A's right hand downwards away with the back of the left hand/left forearm,

13. bringing the right hand clockwise further

14. and taking over holding the wrist now with the right hand
15. and applying a twisting bent hand lock.
16. With a little jerk, A grabs hold of D's right thumb
17. and applies a finger lock.
18. D strikes A's right arm with the back of the left hand/left forearm downwards and away
19. and directly applies a twisting stretched lock.
20. A angles his arm again and applies a bent arm lock on D.
21. D avoids this by delivering a punch with the ball of the hand at A's right shoulder. The turning point was with No. 21 and this can only be done further by executing No. 2 in the locking sequence.

Stretched arm lock

Attacker's actions/Follow-on by the defender

- A pulls his right arm in the direction of his right shoulder.
- D applies a bent arm lock.

- A pulls his right arm in the direction of his left shoulder.
- D pushes A's elbow upwards in the direction of A's face and forces him down to the ground with a stretched arm lock.

- A turns his right wrist over so that flat of the hand is pointing upwards.
- D applies a bent wrist lock.

- A bends his arm and pulls it downwards.
- D applies a twisting hand lock.

- A pulls his arm in the direction of his upper body ('Z' shape).
- D applies a twisting hand lock.

Bent arm lock

Attacker's actions
A stretches out his right arm

Follow-on by the defender
D applies a stretched lock over the body

A stretches out his right arm

D applies a stretched arm lock

A stretches out his right arm

D applies a stretched lock over the stomach

Attacker's actions

- A stretches out his right arm and turns it over.

Follow-on by the defender

- D applies a twisting stretch lock.

Bent hand lock

Attacker's actions/Follow-on by the defender

- A knocks D's right hand in the direction of his left shoulder.
- D lets go of the right wrist and grabs hold of the left wrist and applies a stretched arm lock with support from the right hand (on A's left elbow).

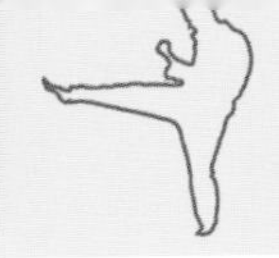

- A knocks D's right hand away downwards with his left hand.
- D makes use of the energy bringing his right hand round counterclockwise inwards and applies a bent arm lock.

- A turns his hand counterclockwise.
- D applies a bent wrist lock.

- A stretches out his arm.
- D applies a stretched arm lock.

- A turns his hand clockwise.
- D applies a twisting hand lock.

11.2 Follow-on techniques after a defended Atemi technique by the defender (Trapping)

- The pupil defends himself in the course of the defending actions by using an Atemi technique of his own choosing (e.g., strike with the edge of the hand).
- The defender's Atemi technique is stopped or diverted (by defensive measures or holding)–the use of various Atemi techniques is possible.
- On his part, the defender executes two different follow-on techniques designed to disrupt (e.g., knocking away or locking the defending arm).
- The pupil can discuss the situation with his partner beforehand to prepare for his demonstration.

This section in the Jiu-Jitsu program is called, for example, in the Philippines System "Trapping".

In Jeet Kune Do (JKD), these types of techniques are called 'hand immobilization attacks'. The techniques are well-known from Wing Tsun (WT) (sometimes spelled differently) and JKD. Bruce Lee, the founder of JKD, was a pupil of Yip Man, who made WT well-known. Anyone who has trained or fought at this distance with athletes from this type of sport will have to admit, that it is very difficult to come out on top, as long as one does not have any specific knowledge of this area. Just as I personally consider that these techniques at this distance from JKD and WT are so effective, I wish that in future they will gain more recognition for inclusion in the Jiu-Jitsu grading program.

In the following sections I will give a brief introduction of the techniques, that will serve to cover the requirements of the grading program. I have also used the terminology

used in JKD/WT. I did not want to just simply say "knock away" or other simplistic words, because the techniques are a large element also in other types of martial arts or systems.

In all the attacks carried out by D, these could be preceded with a sideways kick at the shinbone. This represents a typical sequence and method (attack low attack high) in Jeet Kune Do.

Pak Sao—also known as "slapping hand"—is used when A:

- Uses no or little pressure when blocking.

Application:

1. A punches with his left fist. D sweeps the arm inwards with his right hand.
2. A punches with his right fist. D sweeps the arm inwards with his left hand.
3. D delivers a finger jab at A's eyes with his right hand. A parries with a right forearm block outwards.
4. D knocks A's right arm inwards with his left hand (Pak Sao)...
5. ...and, without having pulled the right hand back first, delivers a right-fisted punch at A's chin.
6. D 'flaps' the right arm downwards and takes hold of A's triceps with his right hand and then presses his right elbow against A's upper body and the left elbow (Gum Sao)...
7. ...and ends the combination with a left-fisted punch at A's chin.

1

2
3
4
5
6
7

1. A delivers a right-fisted punch. D sweeps the arm inwards with his left hand.
2. D delivers a right-fisted punch at A's stomach.
   A carries out a forearm block downwards and outwards to the right.
3. D knocks A's right arm inwards with his left hand (Pak Sao)...
4. ...and delivers a right-arm slap with the back of the hand at A's head.
5. D 'flaps' the right arm downwards and takes hold of A's right triceps with his right hand and then presses his right elbow against A's upper body and A's left arm (Gum Sao)...
6. ...and ends the combination with a left-fisted punch at A's chin.

Lop Sao—also known as "grabbing hand"—is used when A:

- Exerts pressure on the right shoulder when blocking.
- In WT (spelled also differently), generally, grabbing hold actions are not carried out, rather, for example, a strike with the ball of the hand is done.
- A's wrist could also be taken hold of in order, for example, to apply a locking technique.
- Smaller/not so strong defenders tend not to pull A's arm so much, but rather move themselves round A.

The action of pulling on A's arm towards the own hip, so that A cannot counter with an elbow strike, is not carried out; it is more pulled away from the body.

Application:

1. A delivers a right-fisted punch at D's head. D sweeps the arm inwards with his left hand.
2. D delivers a right-Handkantenschlag at A's head. A blocks the punch with the right forearm, exercising a lot of pressure in the direction of D's right shoulder.
3. If D is stronger than A, he pulls A's right arm down with his right hand (not close to the body, otherwise A would be able to counter with an elbow strike at the chest).
   If D is weaker, he pulls the hand and moves round A and delivers a left-fisted punch at A's head...
4. placing the left forearm on A's right elbow and applying a stretched arm lock.

Jao Sao—also known as "running hand"—is used when D wants to change the line of attack:

- From the inside outwards.
- From the outside inwards.
- From low down to high up.
- From high up to low down.

Application:

1. A delivers a right-fisted punch at D's head. D sweeps the arm inwards with his left hand.
2. D delivers a clip of the ear with his left hand at A's head.
   A blocks this with his right arm outwards.
3. D punches in a circling motion clockwise round A's right arm inwards and strikes A's stomach.
4. D's left hand strikes (Pak Sao) A's right hand at elbow height on A's body.
   At the same time, he rolls the right hand clockwise through underneath A's right hand and delivers a strike with the back of the hand at A's head.

Jut Sao—also known as "jerking hand" or "short snapping hand"—is used in order to pull A's cover down:

Application:

1. A delivers a right-fisted punch at D's head. D sweeps the arm inwards with his left hand.

2. D delivers a clip of the ear with his right hand at A's head.
A blocks this with a left forearm block outwards.

3. With his right hand, D grabs hold of A's forearm and pulls this down (like the handle on a slot machine) delivering at the same time a left-fisted punch at A's chin.

4. D 'flaps' the left arm inwards round A's left elbow and then presses his left elbow against A's upper body and A's right arm (Gum Sao)...

5. ...and ends the combination with a punch at A's chin.

Application:

1. A delivers a punch at D's head. D sweeps A's right arm inwards with his left hand.
2. D delivers a clip of the ear with his right hand at A's head.
   A blocks this with a left forearm block outwards.
3. D grabs hold on top of A's forearm with both hands and pulls them down (like the handle on a slot machine) executing a head butt at A at the same time...
4. D 'flaps' the left arm inwards round A's left elbow and then presses his left elbow against A's upper body and A's right arm (Gum Sao)...
5. ...and ends the combination with a punch at A's chin.

Huen Sao—also known as "circling hand"—is used in order to execute a small circular movement:

- From outwards to the inside.
- From inwards to outside.

Application:

1. A delivers a punch at D's head. D counters by making a hand sweep inwards with his right hand.
2. D delivers a clip of the ear with his right hand at A's head.
   A blocks this with a left forearm block outwards.
3. With his right hand, D winds it close round inside A's left forearm (like a snake)...
4. ...and delivers a finger jab at the hollow of A's larynx.
5. D hits the right arm to the middle of A's body with the left hand (Pak Sao)...
6. ...at the same time brings his right arm clockwise underneath A's right arm outwards and delivers a strike with the back of the hand at A's head.

Tan Sao—also known as "begging hand"—is used when A is executing a counter technique in the direction of D's left shoulder:

Application:

1. A delivers a punch at D's head. D counters by making a hand sweep inwards with his left hand.
2. D delivers a finger jab at A's eyes with his right hand.
   A blocks this with a right forearm block outwards, exercising strong pressure in the direction of D's left shoulder.
3. D brings the left hand underneath his own right hand and A's right hand lays the back of the left hand on A's right forearm (as if he were carrying a tray) and brings A's right arm outwards.
4. D delivers a strike with the edge of his right hand (without pulling it back first) at the right side of A's neck.

All the examples can be continued using follow-on combinations. The trapping techniques serve as a transition between boxing distance and throwing distance (grappling).

11.3 Follow-on techniques after a throw technique

- A follow-on each from two, freely selected by the pupil, throwing techniques, carried out after the attacker's reaction.
- For the follow-on, the energy used by the opponent in his reaction should be used in the defense further.

Hip Throw

Attacker's actions	**Defender's actions**
A dodges back to the left	D counters with major inner reaping throw
A jumps backwards	D counters with a sweeping hip throw
A dodges to the right	D counters with a minor inner reaping throw
A pushes his hips forward and supports himself	D counters with a major outer reaping throw
A tries to counter with his own hip throw	D runs round A and throws him in spite of this with a hip throw
A runs in front of D	D counters with directional throw

Major Outer Reaping Throw

Attacker's actions	**Defender's actions**
A lifts the right leg up and turns round 90° backwards	D counters with a directional throw
A lifts the right leg up and turns round 90° backwards	D counters with a sweeping hip throw or an inner thigh throw
A lifts the right leg up and turns round 90° backwards	D counters with a body throw
A jumps back with both feet	D counters with a loin wheel throw

Minor Inner Reaping Throw

Attacker's actions	**Defender's actions**
A backs out with the right leg rearwards	D counters with a major inner reaping throw
A jumps back with both legs and supports himself	D counters with a directional or a head throw

Hip throw — Major inner reaping throw

Hip throw — Sweeping hip throw

Hip throw — Major outer reaping throw

Hip throw — Hip throw

Hip throw—Directional throw

Major outer reaping throw—Directional throw

Major outer reaping throw—Sweeping hip throw

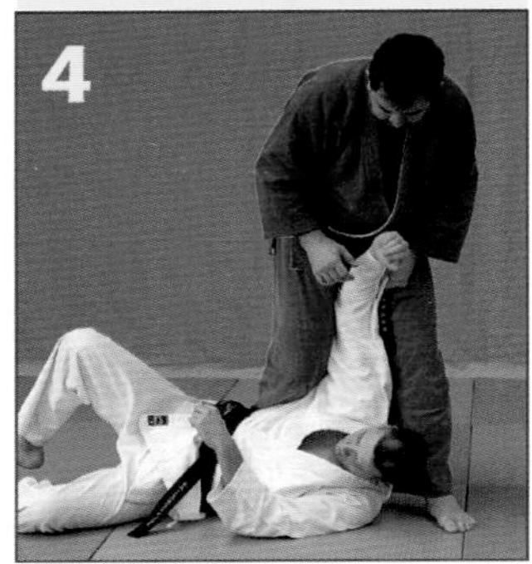

Major outer reaping throw — Body throw

Major outer reaping throw — Directional throw

Minor inner reaping throw—Major inner reaping throw

Minor inner reaping throw—Head throw

12 Counter Measure Techniques

12.1 Counter measures against locking techniques

- A counter measure technique each against two attacking locks freely selected by the pupil.
- For the execution of the counter measure, the energy used by the opponent in his reaction should be used in the pupil's own defense further.

This point was also covered in the sections on the sequence of locking actions—Chapter 11 "Follow-on Techniques" .

Attacker's actions	**Defender's counter measure**
• Stretched arm lock	Stretched arm lock over the upper arm

4

Attacker's actions

- Stretched arm lock over the shoulder

Defender's counter measure

Sword throw

Attacker's actions

- Twisting stretch lock

Defender's counter measure

Bent arm lock

Attacker's actions

- Bent wrist lock

Defender's counter measure

Bent wrist lock

Attacker's actions

- Bent wrist lock

Defender's counter measure

Twisting stretched arm lock

Attacker's actions

- Twisting bent hand lock

Defender's counter measure

Finger lock

Attacker's actions

- Stretched arm lock over the stomach

Defender's counter measure

Excavator throw

12.2 Counter measures against throwing techniques

- A counter measure technique each against two throwing techniques freely selected by the pupil.
- For the execution of the counter measure, the energy used by the opponent in his reaction should be used in the pupil's own defense further.

Attacker's actions	Defender's actions
Hip throw	Left hip throw
Major outer reaping throw	Major outer reaping throw
Major outer reaping throw	Minor inner reaping throw
Two-handed reaping throw	Bale throw
Hip throw	Side-wheel reap
Hip throw	Fall throw
Body throw	Minor outer hooking leg

Hip throw—Left hip throw

Major outer reaping throw—Major outer reaping throw

Major outer reaping throw—Minor outer reaping throw

Two-handed reaping throw—Bale throw

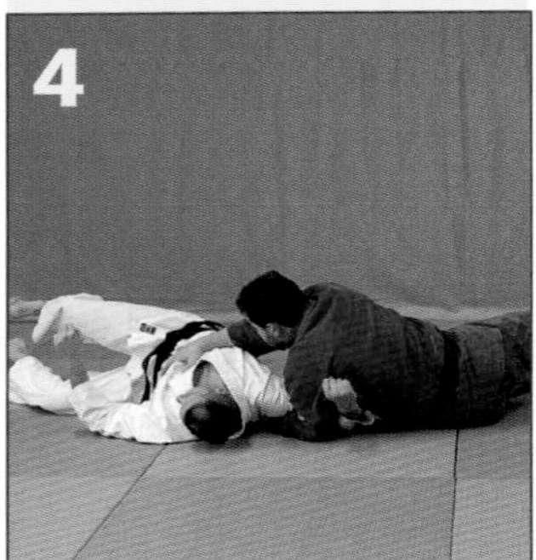

Hip throw—Side wheel reap

Hip throw—Fall throw

Body throw — Minor outer hooking leg

13 Free Self-defense

Five Bear-hug attacks (Duo Series 2)

- Defense options according to ability of the pupil.
- The pupil can decide which defense technique he will use.
- The attacks should be carried out dynamically with defense actions following on immediately.

Attention should be paid to effectiveness, dynamics, correct reach distance and general impression.

13.1 Free self-defense against bear-hugging techniques

13.1.1 Attack No. 1—Frontal hug underneath the arms

1. A hugs hold of D frontally under the arms.
2. D 'rubs' both of his thumbs over A's eyes...
3. ...and grabs hold of A's head by the neck delivers a head butt at A's head followed by a knee kick at the abdomen.

4. D places the left hand under A's neck and the right hand on his chin and pushes the head down into the neck.

5. After this, A is forced down in the direction of the ground with this neck lock.

6-8. A rain of fist punches at A's head ends the combination.

1. A hugs hold of D frontally under the arms.
2. D exerts extreme pressure on A's ears with both hands...
3. ...grabs hold of A's head by the neck with the left hand and the chin with the right hand and pushes the head down into the neck...
4. ...carrying out a neck lock down to the ground...
5. ...and ends the combination with an arm lock (stretched arm lock).

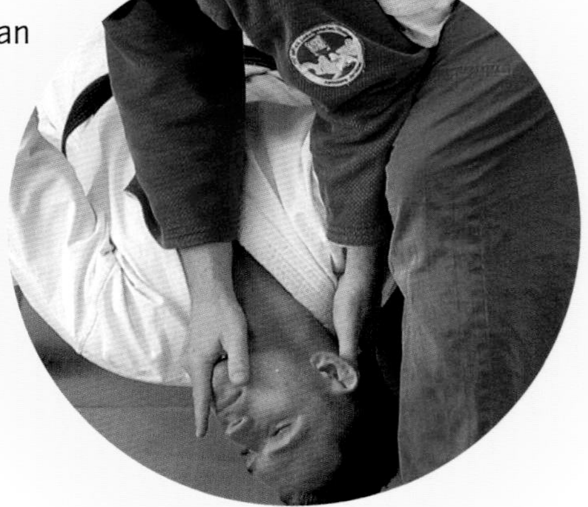

1. A hugs hold of D frontally under the arms.
   D clenches his fists with the thumb over the fingers...
2. ...and delivers a punch with the thumb side of the fist into A's kidneys.
3. D places the left hand on A's lower back and his right hand under the chin...
4. ...and forces A down to the ground by bending him over his back.
5. D kneels on A's neck and the right side of his body and ends the combination by immobilizing him with a bent arm lock.

13.1.2 Attack No. 2 – Frontal hug trapping the arms

1. A hugs hold of D, trapping ths arms.
2. D places both hands on A's pelvis and pushes both arms to downwards and forwards...
3. ...while delivering a knee kick at the genitals.
4. D's left hand is 'wrapped' round A's right arm, which is placed in the elbow joint. D's left hand is placed on his right hand so that a twisting stretch lock is applied (stretched arm lock).

2

3

1

4

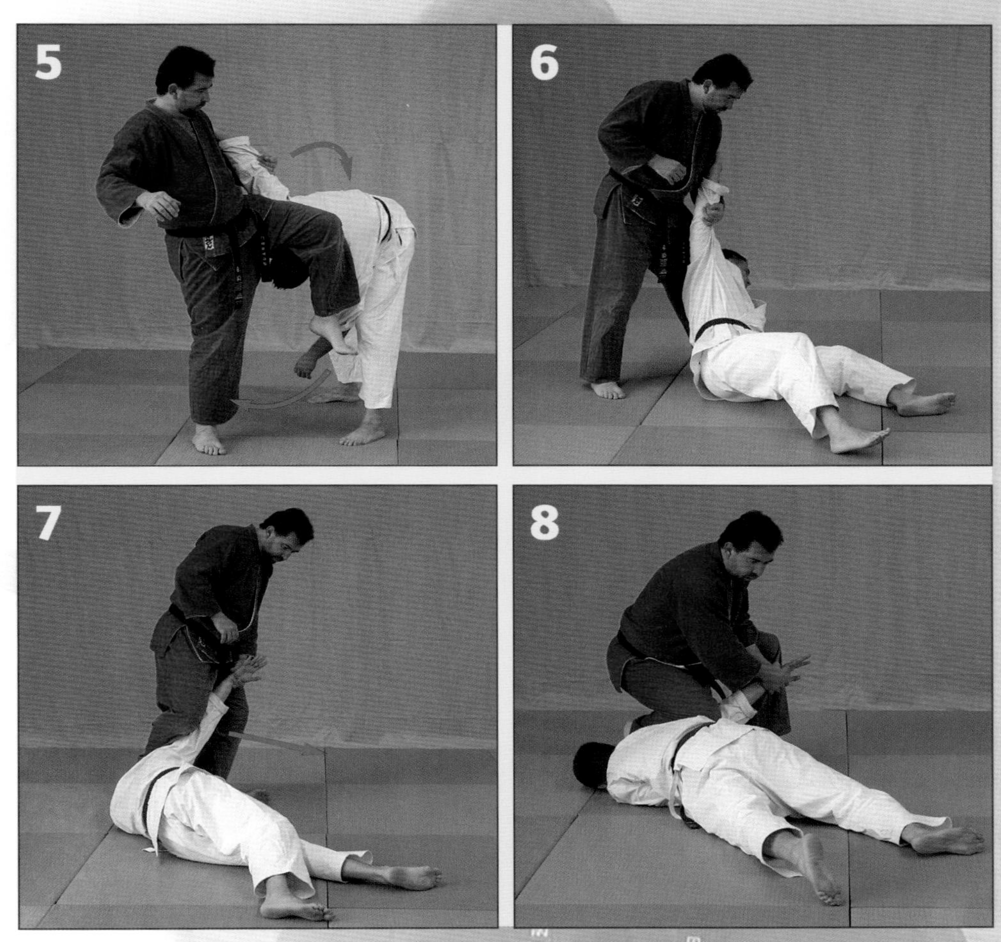

5. D brings his left leg over A's head...
6. ...and executes a twisting throw.
7. After this he places his right foot on A's upper arm...
8. ...and turns A over onto his stomach ending the combination with a stretched arm lock.

1. A hugs hold of D frontally trapping ths arms.
2. D delivers a head butt.
3. By stretching both arms he frees himself from the bear hug.
4. The right hand is placed along A's right groin and the left hand grabs hold of the right ankle.
5. By pulling the foot and pushing on the groin (45° to the rear) A is forced to fall over.
6. D executes a leg lock, fixing the left by placing his right foot on the thigh.

1. A hugs hold of D frontally trapping ths arms.
2. D stamps down on A's left foot with his right foot...
3. ...grabs round A's back in a hug with both arms bringing his head underneath A's chin.
4. By applying pressure on A's spine and chin, A is forced to hollow his back and is brought over onto the ground.
5. D adopts the straddle position, pushing his legs under A's legs.
6. D places his right lower arm under A's neck.
   - D places his right hand on the left biceps...
   - ...and the left hand on the right side of A's face.
   - D lays his own right side of the face onto the back of his left hand.
   - The shoulders are placed under and in front of A's jaw.
   - By applying pressure forwards D applies a neck lock.

13.1.3 Attack No. 3—Side headlock

1. A takes hold of D with a sideways headlock.
2. D presses his left thumb in A's right eye.
   A loosens his grip and stands up.
3. D grabs hold of A's testicles with his right hand and pulls them up...
4. ...forcing A to fall over backwards.
   By applying pressure to the nerve point in A's eye, he is immobilized on the ground.

1. A takes hold of D with a sideways headlock.
D reaches round A's head with his left arm, and pokes the middle finger of the left hand into A's left eye causing A to loosen his grip and stand up.
D grabs hold of A's right hand with his right hand...

2-3. ...and pulls his head out of the 'noose'...

4. ...and then bends the right arm over his back to apply a bent arm lock (to be able to move A about).

1. A takes hold of D with a sideways headlock.
2. D presses his left thumb into A's right eye.
3-4. A loosens his grip and stands up. D executes a backwards throw on A...
5. ...and immediately adopts the straddle position...
6-7. ...ending the combination using a side stretch lock (stretched arm lock).

13.1.4 Attack No. 4—Frontal headlock

1. A takes hold of D with a frontal headlock.

2. D delivers a hand jab at A's neck/Adam's apple. This causes A to loosen his grip and arch his back...

3. ...this is followed by executing a variation of the two-handed crescent sweep like e.g., taught in the Luta-Livre.
D kneels on his right knee in front of A having placed his left leg next to A's right leg. D grabs round both legs at the height of the hollows of the knees and pulls them together so they form an 'X'.

4. By pressing against the legs D causes A to fall over backwards...

5-6. ...and then goes immediately into the crossover position.
He ends the combination with a bent arm lock.

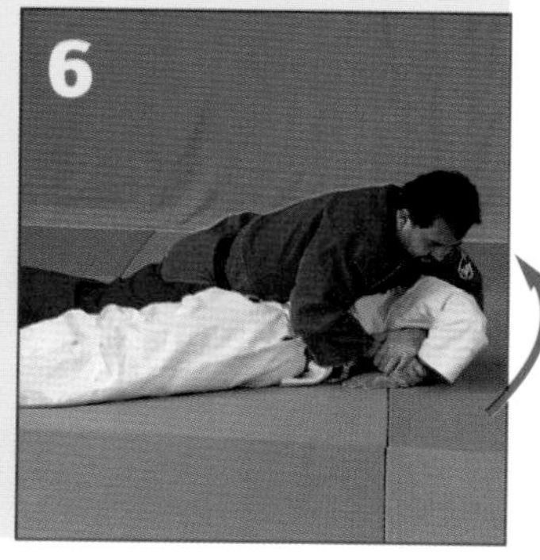

1. A takes hold of D with a frontal headlock.
2. D delivers a hand jab with his right hand at A's neck/Adam's apple...
3. ...while at the same time grabbing his testicles with the left hand.
4. By applying pressure on the neck/Adam's apple and pulling the testicles A is forced down backwards.
5. D gets into a side position (on the left hand side of A) and grabs hold of A's right wrist with his right hand pushes his left arm through under A's right arm and takes hold of his own right wrist then he twists his wrist upwards (like accelerating on a motor-bike) pulls A's elbow to the right hip and bends the elbow upwards and immobilizes A with a bent arm lock.

1. A takes hold of D with a frontal headlock.
2. D delivers a hand jab with his right hand at A's neck/Adam's apple... This causes A to loosen his grip and arch his back.
3. D grabs hold of A's right wrist with his left hand and pulls it downwards (opens the grip correctly)...
4. ...ducks under A's right arm...
5. ...and bends A's arm up behind his back...
6. ...gouging A's eyes from behind with his right hand and transports A about moving him with the bent arm lock.

13.1.5 Attack No. 5–Strangling from behind using the forearm

1. A takes hold of D with a strangling grip from behind with the forearm.
2. D grabs hold of A's right wrist.
   D takes a step backwards to the right in order to get into a forward leaning stance...
3. ...delivers an elbow strike rearwards with his left arm...
4. ...bends the left forearm down to deliver a fist punch at A's genital area...

5. ...extends the thumb out on the left hand 'bends' the left arm back up again and delivers a finger stab at A's eyes.

6. D frees himself from the hold round his neck using his right arm...

7. ...ducks through under the right arm rearwards and then is on the outside of A.

8. D brings the arm further round on to A's back (bent arm lock to transport A) gouging A's eyes from behind with his left hand.

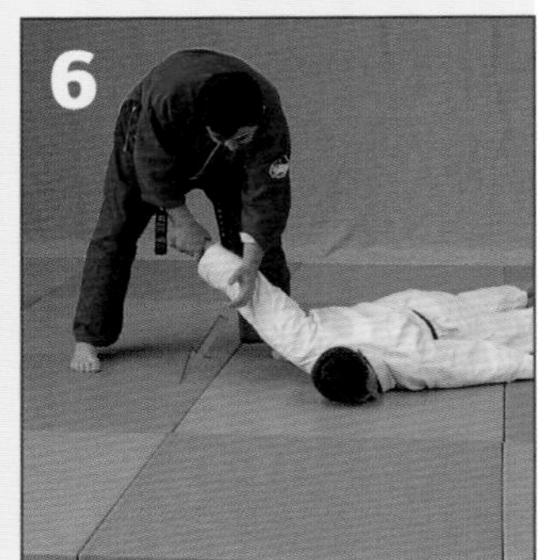

1. A takes hold of D with a strangling grip from behind with the forearm.
2. D grabs hold of A's right wrist with his right hand.
   D takes a step backwards to the right in order to get into a forward leaning stance...
3. ...delivers a hammer strike at A's genitals...
4. ...and ducks through under A's right arm...
5. ...and places the left arm on A's right elbow...
6. ...bringing A down to the ground with a stretched arm lock.
7. D immobilizes A with a bent hand lock, kneeling down with his left knee between A's shoulder blades.

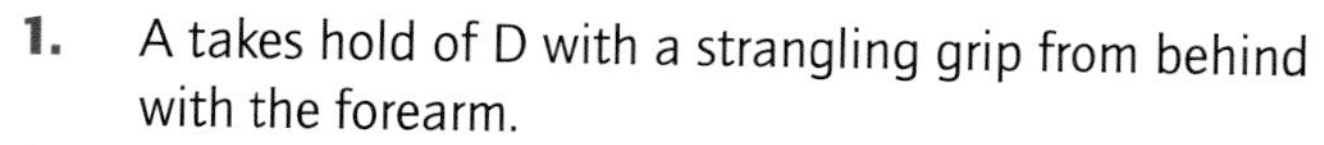

1. A takes hold of D with a strangling grip from behind with the forearm.
2. D gouges A's eye with his left thumb rips A's right arm down a little with his left arm...
3. ...and then turns to the right so that his own Adam's apple is lying in A's elbow joint and grabs A in the face with his right hand followed by grabbing the joint of A's right elbow placing his right leg behind A's right leg and executing a trip throw.

4-5. D pushes A's head over to the left side with his left hand...

6. ...and climbs over A's body, first with the left foot and then the right one...
7. ...ending the combination with a side stretch lock (stretched arm lock). Here, D keeps his knees firmly together, lifts his hips and pulls the right arm over his groin with the little finger pointing down to the floor. His toes are placed well under A's left arm so that he cannot grab hold of them.

13.2 Free self-defense against Atemi attacks

- Defense options according to ability of the pupil.
- The pupil can decide which defense technique he will use.
- The attacks should be carried out dynamically with defense actions following on immediately. All attacks are executed with the right foot leading.

Attention should be paid to effectiveness, dynamics, correct reach distance and general impression.

13.2.1 Attack No 1—Right-fisted punch at the head (right foot leading)

1. D sweeps the punch away down to the left outside with his left arm...
2. ...and delivers an elbow strike at A's head with his right elbow...
3. ...'wraps' the left arm round A's right arm to apply a twisted stretch lock (stretched arm lock) and then presses the head 45° forwards and downwards with his right hand.

1

2

3

4. D swings his left leg over A's head

5. and forces him down to the ground by the leg with a swinging throw.

6. A crescent swinging kick at the head ends the combination.

1-2. A delivers a right-fisted punch at D's head.
D sweeps the arm away to the left and outside.

3. This is followed by a sword hand strike with the right hand coming in from the left side at the right-hand side of A's neck.

4. The right hand pushes the head to the side...

5. ...and a left elbow strike is delivered at the right side of the neck.

6. The left hand is bent up and, coming in from the left-hand side of the neck, laid on the nape of the neck.

7. D pulls the neck down onto a knee strike carried out using the left one.

8. A right cross punch at the chin ends the combination.

1-2. A delivers a right-fisted punch at D's head.
D sweeps the punch away with a left-right to the outside right...

3. ...and delivers a sword hand strike at A's neck/head.

4. As he does this, D grabs hold of A's right wrist with his right hand...

5. ...bends A's right arm inwards and with his left hand he takes hold of his own right wrist applies a bent arm lock in the direction of the ground and simultaneously in the same movement he delivers an elbow strike at A's chin.

6. A is immobilized on the ground with a bent hand lock. To do this D kneels down on A's neck with his left knee and his right knee at A's side.

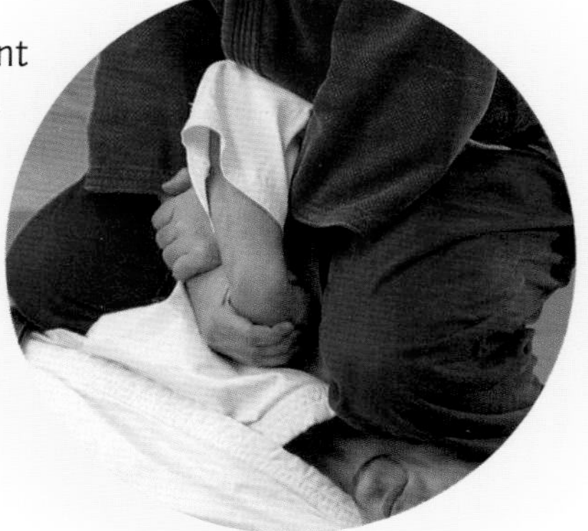

13.2.2 Attack No. 2—Right-fisted punch (left leg leading) at the middle of the body

1. A delivers a right-fisted punch to the center of the body.
2. D carries out a passive block to the inside with his left arm...
3. ...sweeps the arm using his left arm downwards and outwards, while delivering a finger jab at A's eyes then wraps the left arm round A's right arm and applies a twisting stretch lock...
4. ...forcing A to the ground and immobilizing him.

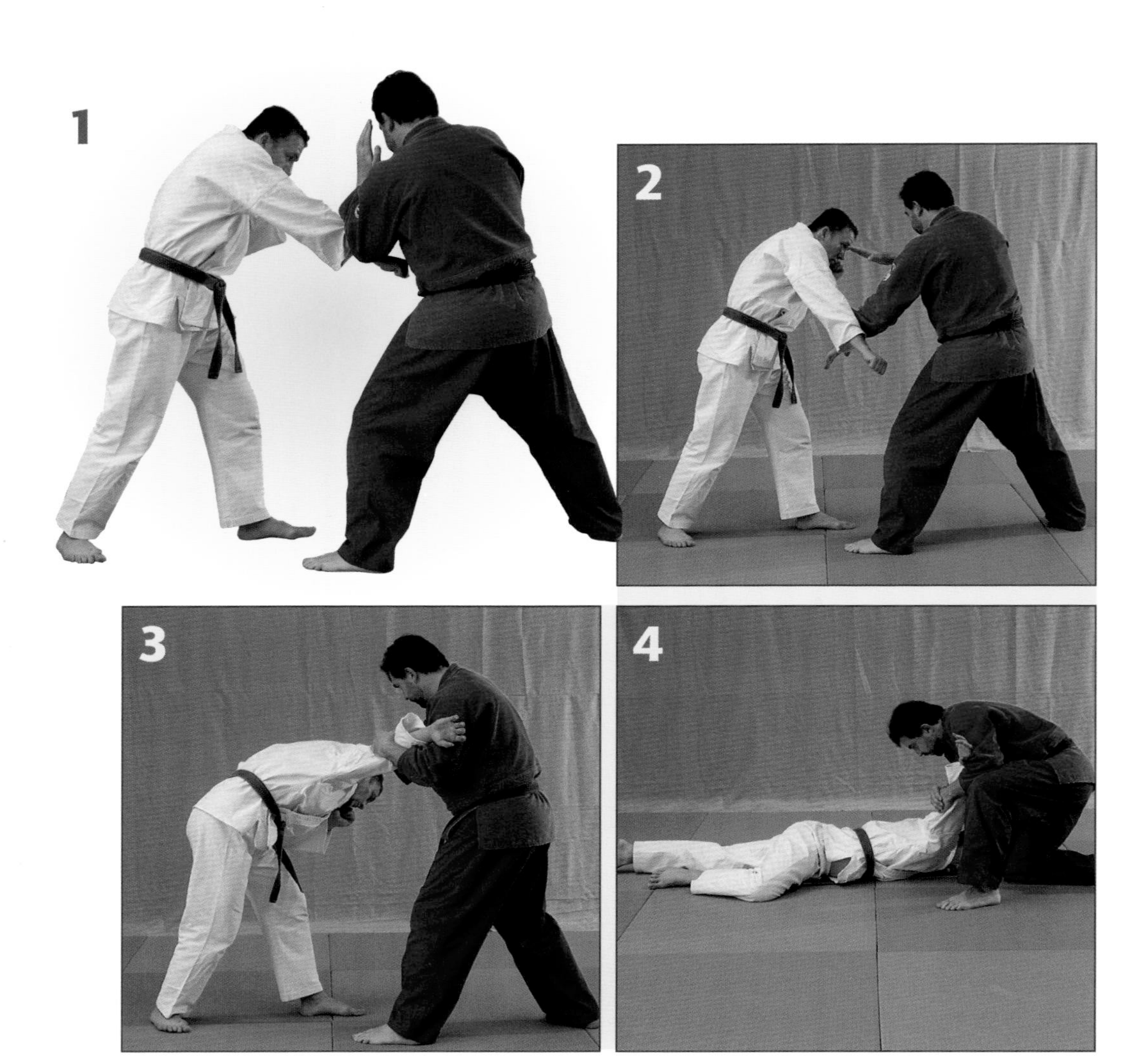

1-2. A delivers a right-fisted punch to the center of the body.
D carries out a right forearm block downwards and outwards strikes A's right elbow with his left hand (Pak Sao) and traps it against A's upper body.

3. At the same time, D delivers a backhanded strike with his right hand at A's head.

4. The right hand/right arm is laid crosswise over both of A's arms i.e., thus blocking the arms temporarily (Gum Sao) and then he delivers a left-fisted punch at A's chin.

1-2. A delivers a right-fisted punch to the center of the body.
D carries out a right forearm block downwards and outwards while at the same time delivering a left-handed finger jab at the eyes then, grabs hold of A's right elbow with the thumb and middle finger of the left hand just above the elbow...

3. ...pulls the arm while delivering a right elbow strike at A's right biceps (Sandwich).

4. The right hand is bent down and grabs the upper arm pulling it upwards.

5. D delivers a left-fisted punch at the lower ribcage.

6. The right elbow sweeps the right upper arm downwards.

7. D rubs the right thumb over A's right eye...

8. ...and ends the combination with a left-fisted punch at A's chin.

13.2.3 Attack No. 3—Sword hand strike with the right hand (leading with the left foot) at the neck

1. A delivers a sword hand strike with the right hand at D's neck.
2-3. D carries out a three step contact (block left—sweep outwards with the right—control the elbow with the left) blocking the right arm outwards to the right...
4. ...also grabbing hold of A's right arm with his right hand...

5. ...pulling A's arm hard with both of his arms, delivering at the same time a head butt (with the top of the skull) at A's head.

6. D places the left hand in A's lumbar region and his right hand on A's chin...

7. ...and forces A over backwards onto the ground.

8. D kneels on A's neck with the other knee at A's side and immobilizes him with a bent arm lock.

1. A delivers a sword hand strike with the right hand at D's neck.
D sweeps the arm to the left and outside and brings his hand across to his left hip...

2. ...and takes over holding A's right arm with the left hand.

3. D delivers a right arm sword hand strike, coming in from the left side, at the liver/lower ribcage...

4. ...and places the middle finger of the right hand in A's right elbow joint...

5-6. ...and pulls him down to the ground with a bent arm lock.
D pulls on the wrist with his left hand and pushes against A's right elbow with his right hand so that A arches his back from pain.
D then just immobilizes A on the ground with the stretched arm (stretched arm lock).

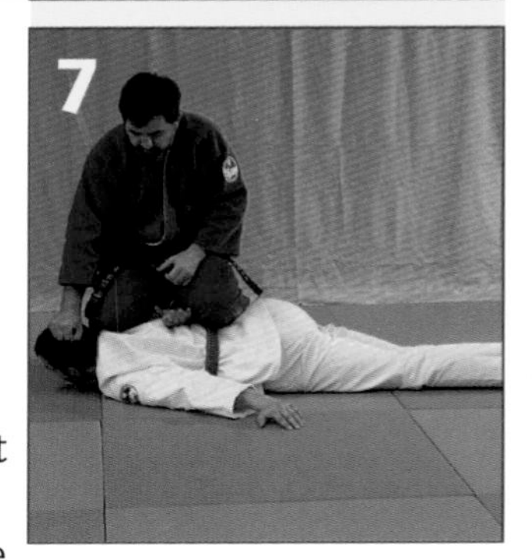

1. A delivers a sword hand strike with the right hand at D's neck.
   D sweeps the sword hand attack diagonally to the right and outwards with his right arm...
2. ...at the same time delivering a left-handed finger jab at A's eyes...
3. ...taking over holding A's right hand with his left hand...
4. ...then takes a step turn 90° backwards...
5. ...and forces A down to the ground with a bent wrist lock (carried out using the right elbow).
6. D turns A over onto his stomach...
7. ...angles the right arm up for a bent arm lock on A's back and kneels down with both knees on A's back.

13.2.4 Attack No. 4 — Frontal kick at the middle of the body

1. A kicks out at the middle of D's body.

2-3. D carries out a defensive technique using his right lower leg outwards to the right...

4. ...making a 90° step turn backwards and then grabs hold of A's right shoulder with his right hand...

5-6. ...throwing A with a major outer reaping throw.

1

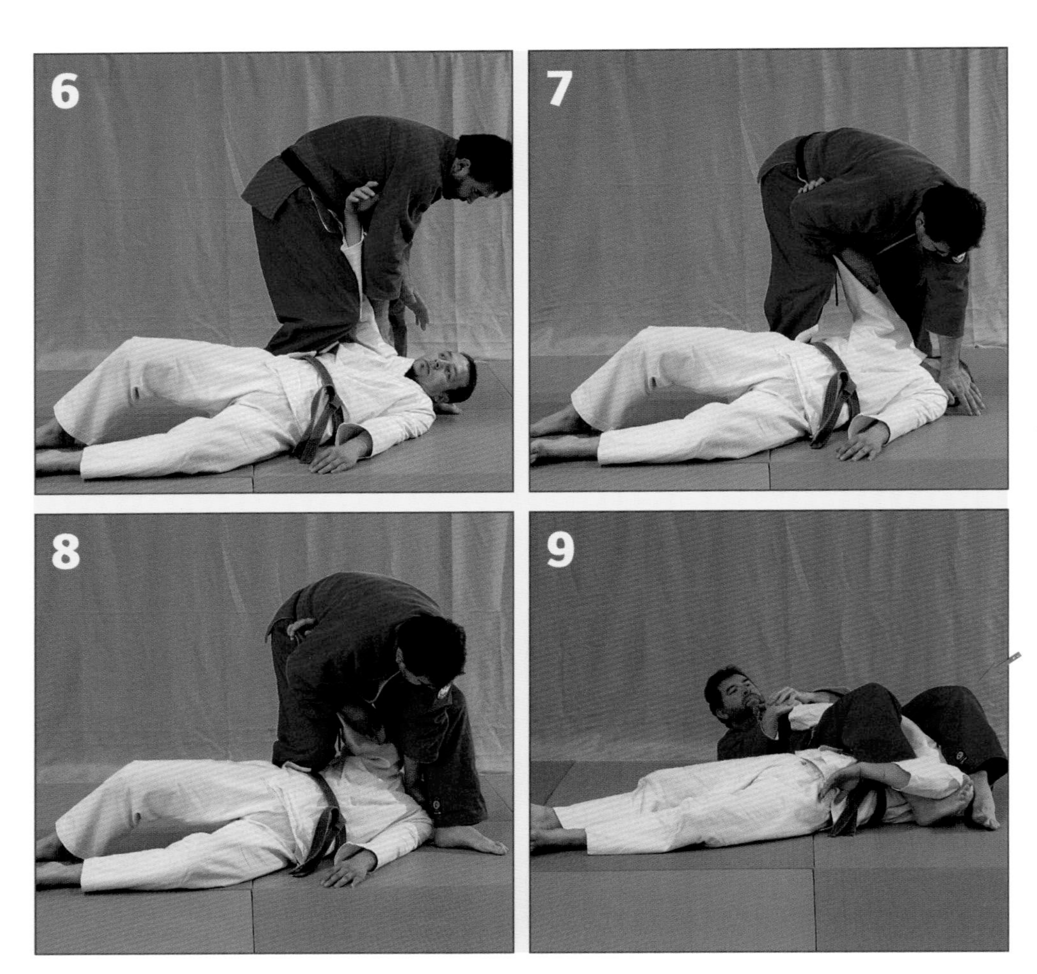

7. D presses A's face to the ground with the left hand...

8. ...and places his left leg over past A's head.

9. D immobilizes A on the ground with a side stretch lock (stretched arm lock).

1. A kicks out at the middle of D's body.
D delivers a right elbow strike downwards on A's shinbone...

2. ...and then grabs hold of A's head with both hands, with the thumbs gouging A's eyes...

3. ...delivering a head butt...

4. ...followed by a left knee strike to the head.

5. D turns the head to the left, and by doing this, forces A down to the ground...

6-8. ...ending the combination with a rain of punches at A's head.

1-2. A kicks out at the middle of D's body.
D carries out a defensive technique using his left lower leg outwards to the right...

3. ...followed by a left-fisted punch at A's stomach (with a lot of weight put behind it) and doing a 45° lunge step forwards to the right at the same time.

4. The right hand is covering D's own head as he does this.

5. The left hand grabs hold of A's left hand and pulls the arm forward (Lop Sao)...

6. ...and the right hand delivers a punch at A's head.

7-8. With the right forearm, pressure is applied to A's left elbow joint and A is forced down to the ground with a stretched arm lock.

13.2.5 Attack No. 5 — Frontal crescent kick at the middle of the body

1. As the kick comes in D delivers a kick with his left shinbone at the inside of the thigh...
2. ...followed by a right-fisted punch at the chin...
3. ...and a left uppercut at the chin.
4. D turns in front of A and lays the right arm round the neck as he does...

5. ...bends forward and hooks behind the left leg from the outside with his left foot...
6. ...and carries out a leg roll throw (Sambo roll)...
7-8. ...immobilizing A with a stretched leg lock.

1. A delivers a frontal crescent kick at the middle of the body.
D makes a feint towards the outside right...

2. ...and catches hold underneath A's leg with his left arm.
He then applies pressure to A's right shoulder to cause him to lean over backwards...

3. ...and delivers two knee kicks at A's right thigh...

4-5. ...followed by a right shinbone kick (low kick) at A's left standing leg.

1. A delivers a frontal crescent kick at the middle of the body.
2. With his right hand, D sweeps the leg diagonally to the right and outwards. The left hand is covering his head.
3. After this a right-fisted punch is delivered at A's head...
4. ...and a left-fisted in-swinging punch at A's kidneys.
5. D places both middle fingers into A's groin from behind
6. and pulls A 45° downwards.
7. This causes A to fall over backwards.
   A crescent kick at the head ends the combination.

13.3 Free self-defense using a stick

- The pupil uses a stick (length 50-100cm) to defend himself.
- The defensive actions can be freely chosen, just as the attacking actions are.

1. A executes a bear hug from the side trapping D's arms.
D has the stick in the right hand and brings it round behind A's back...
2. ...taking hold of it with the left hand...
3. ...pulling the grip tight and upwards so that A has to stand on tiptoe.
4. D then throws A with a hip throw forwards.
5-6. A kick with the foot ends the combination.

1. A grabs hold of D's wrist (stick hand) diagonally with his right hand.
2. D 'rolls' the end of the stick (butt end) over A's wrist from the outside.
3. As he does this A's fingers are trapped against D's own wrist.
4. D applies a twisted hand lock...
5. ...holds the butt of the stick in his left hand...
6-7. ...and delivers a strike at A's chin with the butt.

1. A grabs hold of D's wrist (stick hand) diagonally with his right hand.
2. D 'rolls' the end of the stick (butt end) over A's wrist.
3. D's left hand reaches through underneath A's right arm grabs the wrist hard over the stick and applies a hand lock.
4. D lets go of the stick with his right hand (because of the tension on the stick it flies into A's face).

5-6. A circular strike (Rendondo) on A's hand ends the combination.

1. A grabs hold of the wrist (stick hand) diagonally with his right hand.
2. D turns further round in a clockwise direction the left hand takes hold of the right wrist.
3. D carries out a freeing movement with the right hand...

4-5. ...and brings A to the ground with a bent hand lock (over the stick butt).

6-7. Using the stick with a stretched arm lock, A is immobilized on the ground.

1. A grabs hold of the right wrist (stick hand) opposite.
2. D takes hold of the butt of the stick with his left hand...
3. ...and brings the stick clockwise into the horizontal position.

   D pushes against A's hand with the right forearm and applies a hand lock over the stick.

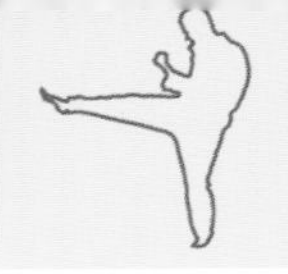

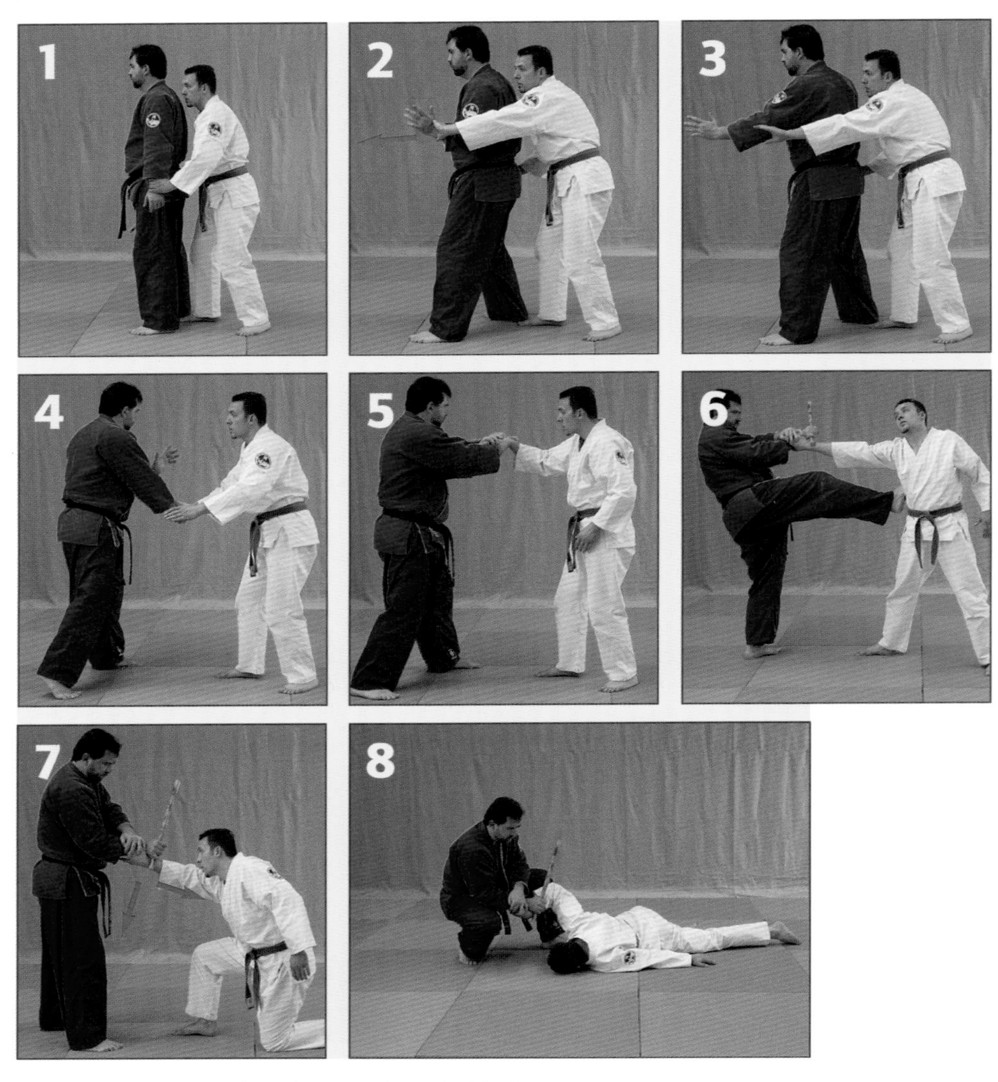

1. A grabs hold of both wrists from behind.
2-3. D frees himself from the grip using the left hand...
4. ...followed by a step turn 180° forwards.
5. D applies a twisted hand lock...
6. ...delivers a kick with the foot at the lower ribcage
7-8. and forces A down to the ground.

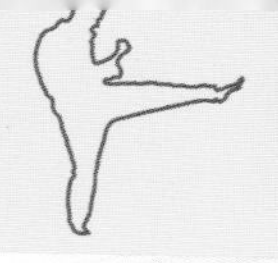

14 Free Applications

14.1 In Atemi

- Standing fighting exclusively using punches and fist strikes.
- Target area is above the belt, glancing contact without having a hard effect on the target.
- Aim: Free application of defensive techniques, forms of movement and fist techniques.
- Protective equipment: Lower protection (for women optional), fist protectors, instep or foot protection, and for children additionally gum-shields (mandatory).
- Length of training time: 1-2 minutes with a change of partners (1x).

14.2 For throwing and groundwork techniques

- Standing fighting, following grip contact on the move.
- Use of throwing techniques, transitions from standing through to groundwork, and groundwork itself.
- Atemi techniques may not be used.
- Protective equipment: Fist protectors, lower protection (for women optional), instep or foot protection, and for children additionally gum-shields (mandatory).
- Length of training time: 1-2 minutes with a change of partners (1x).

Literature

On my Internet web pages under www.open-mind-combat.com a list of books can be found. Those interested can gain an overview of the Martial Arts literature. The publishers of this book, Meyer & Meyer, have a large coverage of publications on the Martial Arts—see their Internet web page under www.m-m-sports.com.

Photo & Illustration Credits

Cover design: Jens Vogelsang
Photos: Christian Braun

About the Author

Christian Braun—born 1965

Address:
Peter-Paul-Rubens-Str 1
67227 Frankenthal
Germany
Email: Christian.Braun@open-mind-combat.com
Web Page: www.open-mind-combat.com

Requests for information regarding courses, books and private training should be sent to the above address.

Qualifications:

- Mastrib Guro Open Mind Combat
- 5th Dan Ju-Jutsu, Licensed JJ-Instructor, Trainer 'B' License
- Phase 6 and Madunong Guro in the IKAEF under Jeff Espinous and Johan Skalberg
- Instructor in Progressive Fighting Systems (Jeet Kune Do Concepts) under Paul Vunak
- Instructor in Luta-Livre License Grade 1 under Andreas Schmidt
- 1st Dan Jiu-Jitsu (German Jiu-Jitsu Association)
- Phase 2 Jun Fan Gung Fu under Ralf Beckmann

Offices held:

- 1990-1991—Trainer and Press Representative for the Ju-Jutsu Section of the Judo Association for the German State of the Pfalz (Rhineland Palatinate)
- 1999-2003—Speaker for the Ju-Jutsu Association (Ju-Jutsu Verband Baden e.V.) in matters for Sport for Seniors and the Disabled
- 1992-today—Head of Section in the Turn- und Gefechtclub 1861 e.V. (German Gymnastics and Fencing Club 1861)

Organization:

- Speaker on the German National Seminar of the DJJV e.V. (German Ju-Jutsu Association)
- Speaker at German National Courses by the DJJV e.V.
- Speaker in the faculty of JJ Instructors Division of the DJJV e.V.

Competition Achievements in the Upper Open Weight Classes:

Between 1988-1991 several place results achieved in the Pfalz Individual Championships with 1st Place taken in 1991. Placed in Third Place, three times in the German South-West Individual Championships.